WILDLIFE RESERVES AND CORRIDORS IN THE URBAN ENVIRONMENT

A Guide to Ecological Landscape Planning and Resource Conservation

by
Lowell W. Adams
and
Louise E. Dove

National Institute for Urban Wildlife
10921 Trotting Ridge Way
Columbia, Maryland 21044

Fish and Wildlife Service
Grant Agreement Number 14–16–0009–88–1208
Phillip Agee, Project Officer

Performed for

Division of Federal Aid
Fish and Wildlife Service
U.S. Department of the Interior
Washington, D.C. 20240

1989

ISBN 0–942015–02–9
Library of Congress Catalog Card Number: 88–61762

Published in 1989 by the National Institute for Urban Wildlife, 10921 Trotting Ridge Way, Columbia, Maryland 21044

Printed in the United States of America by Automated Graphic Systems, White Plains, Md.

CONTENTS

PREFACE

There is need, nationally and internationally, for prudent commitment to both sustained economic development as well as responsible environmental and resource protection. In our view, these are mutually dependent, not mutually exclusive. As evidenced in many developing areas of the world, environmental protection and resource conservation receive low priority under struggling economies. But sustained economic development is dependent upon maintenance of clean air and water, unpolluted soil, and the many associated natural resources.

From this perspective, our primary objectives in preparing the present report are twofold: (1) to review the knowledge base regarding wildlife habitat reserves and corridors in urban and urbanizing areas, and (2) to provide some guidelines and approaches to ecological landscape planning and wildlife conservation in such areas that will help to maintain multiple environmental and societal benefits. We hope the report will be useful to biologists, planners, and landscape architects of federal, state, county, and municipal agencies, and to these professionals employed in the private sector; to developers; to college and university educators and their students; and to other groups and individuals interested in wildlife conservation in urban and urbanizing areas.

The report deals primarily with planning considerations before development, rather than habitat management aspects after development. Chapter 1 highlights public interest in wildlife in metropolitan areas and presents a brief overview of the multiple benefits derived from considering wildlife and associated natural resources in the development process. In Chapter 2, we outline some of the known effects of urbanization on wildlife and wildlife habitat as background for a more detailed review of the scientific literature dealing with habitat reserves and corridors in Chapter 3.

Chapter 3 encompasses an extensive review of the empirical evidence relating to wildlife reserves and corridors, with emphasis on urban areas, but also including nonurban areas in recognition that research dealing with the latter may well have considerable application to the urban environment. The practitioner, understandably, needs numbers: How large must the reserve be? How wide must buffer zones be? And how wide must connecting corridors be? Answers to these, and related, questions are dependent upon many factors, and we review the limited research concerned with such issues, noting that present knowledge only provides partial answers. In addition, we include a section on research needs in hope that such a discussion will help to stimulate further, much–needed work in this important area.

The major focus of Chapter 4 is on how the knowledge base reviewed in Chapter 3 can be applied to the development of conservation schemes for the urban and urbanizing environment, resulting in multiple societal benefits. Guidelines to ecological landscape planning and wildlife conservation are provided, along with specific recommendations.

Chapter 5 presents some specific examples of how various approaches to establishing reserves and corridors have been implemented successfully. Our effort here is to illustrate the broad range of possibilities rather than to document the full extent of such approaches. An approach that works well in one locality may be less appropriate in another. Undoubtedly, there is room for innovation, and we hope our discussion here will stimulate further thought and action.

We gratefully acknowledge the financial assistance of the U.S. Fish and Wildlife Service and the guidance and assistance of Phillip Agee, Project Officer, and Conley Moffett, Chief, Division of Federal Aid. We also thank Gomer E. Jones, President, National Institute for Urban Wildlife, for continued support and encouragement. Many people provided information on the subject in response to a request for assistance we circulated within the professional community. Lynda Garrett, Librarian, U.S. Department of the Interior, Patuxent Wildlife Research Center, was particularly helpful in locating pertinent scientific reports for us. In addition, the following individuals provided helpful comments on earlier drafts of the manuscript: P. Agee, V. Flyger, L.D. Harris, G.E. Jones, D.L. Leedy, and C.S. Robbins. Thanks to all of you.

Lowell W. Adams
Louise E. Dove

Columbia, Maryland
January, 1989

1

INTRODUCTION

What are wildlife reserves and interconnecting corridors and of what value are they in urban and urbanizing landscapes? What is ecological landscape planning and how does one go about undertaking such effort? These are questions on which we will focus in the present report. In the discussion that follows, we view wildlife reserves broadly as consisting of variously–designated areas such as wildlife refuges, wildlife sanctuaries, and wildlife preserves, as well as undesignated areas of differing sizes that meet the basic needs of wildlife (e.g., parks, cemeteries, and community open spaces). Corridors are regarded as narrow, linear strips of habitat that have wildlife value. Examples include powerline, pipeline, railway, and highway rights–of–way; fencerows; hedgerows; riparian strips; and shelterbelts. Our discussion of corridors in the present report focuses on those linear strips of habitat serving as interconnecting links between or among larger habitat areas (i.e., wildlife reserves). Clearly, based on current knowledge and understanding, conservation of wildlife and wildlife habitat in metropolitan and developing areas has interrelated human, ecological, environmental quality, and scientific value.

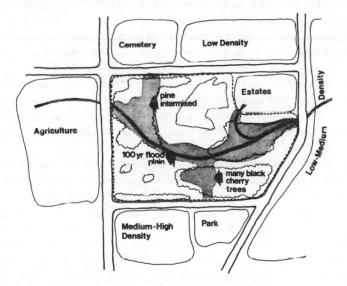

A site sketch with a wildlife corridor (shaded area) linked to surrounding areas. (From Leedy *et al.* 1978.)

There is growing evidence that people living in metropolitan areas are interested in wildlife. For example, in a 1985 national survey of Americans (U.S. Dep. Inter., Fish and Wildlife Serv. and U.S. Dep. Commerce, Bur. of the Census, in press), it was estimated that 58% of Americans (16 years old and over) maintained an active interest in wildlife around the home through such activities as observing, identifying, photographing, and feeding wildlife, or maintaining natural areas or plantings like shrubs and other vegetation for benefit to wildlife. Furthermore, some 65% of the adult population enjoyed seeing or hearing wildlife while pursuing other activities (e.g., lawn care) around the home. A comprehensive survey of Canadians (Filion *et al.* 1983) reported similar results. Some 67% of Canadians (15 years old and over) fed, watched, studied, or photographed wildlife around their homes or cottages (and slightly over 70% of these individuals were urban residents).

Surveys on a smaller scale also have recorded urban resident interest in wildlife. For example, urbanites of Kansas City, Springfield, and St. Louis, Missouri, showed high awareness and enjoyment of urban wildlife— –93% of the respondents described the wild animals around their homes as "enjoyable" rather than "pests," and only 13% reported that they had wildlife–related problems around their residences in the last several years (Witter *et al.* 1981). Gilbert (1982) reported that 90% of the respondents to a survey of residents in Guelph, Ontario felt that the city should be doing more to encourage wildlife conservation, and 46% said they were willing to pay a special municipal tax to support such activities. Other similar studies were reviewed by Adams (1988).

In addition to the human values mentioned above, other socio–economic values are apparent. For example, wildlife reserves and corridors in urban areas can provide opportunities for human recreation and relaxation, and they have aesthetic and educational values. Ninety–six percent of the respondents in a survey of residents of New York City, Buffalo, Rochester, Syracuse, Utica–Rome, and Binghamton, New York indicated that it was important for children to have the opportunity to take part in nature programs beyond those offered in school or at home, and 73% expressed interest in a program to learn how to encourage wildlife to live in their backyard or neighborhood area (Brown *et al.* 1979). (See also Harrison *et al.* 1987.)

Urban reserves and corridors provide ecological and environmental quality values. They help to maintain biological diversity (i.e., the numerous species of plants and animals found throughout the world), thus reducing the threat of species becoming endangered and possibly extinct. Species extinction is of grave concern. Based on review of the scientific evidence, Myers (1988) reported that the present–day extinction rate (due almost entirely to human modification of the landscape) is at least hundreds of times higher than the long–term natural rate. This is alarming because, aside from the ecological roles of species in maintaining functional ecosystems on which all life, including human, depends, we know little about the potential of the vast majority of species for use in medicine, agriculture, and industry. According to Farnsworth and Morris (1976) (as cited in Farnsworth 1988), 25% of all prescriptions dispensed from community pharmacies in the United States over the past 25 years contained active ingredients that are still extracted from higher plants. And, relative to the more than 250,000 species of plants on earth, only a few have been thoroughly studied for their potential value as

Photo: L.W. Adams

Wildlife reserves and corridors in the metropolitan environment have interrelated human, ecological, environmental quality, and scientific value.

a source of useful drugs. Similar arguments can be made for plants and animals in agriculture and industry.

With regard to environmental quality values, trees and shrubs ameliorate the extremes of climate, reduce wind velocity, and reduce the evaporation of soil moisture. Also, plants are useful in landscape architecture, erosion control, watershed protection, wastewater management, noise abatement, and air pollution control.

Reserves and corridors also hold scientific value. In addition to our limited knowledge of the value of plants and animals for use in medicine, agriculture, and industry, there is much to be learned about the structure and function of ecosystems, both disturbed and undisturbed ones. Only from a sound knowledge base will we be able to manage wildlife and other natural resources effectively for their multiple benefits and values.

In recent years, the term "landscape ecology" has gained recognition in the United States. Several recent textbooks (e.g., Vink 1983, Naveh and Lieberman 1984, and Forman and Godron 1986) have assisted this effort. However, according to Vink (1983), the term was introduced in 1938 by the German geographer Carl Troll. The field is concerned both with "natural" landscapes and "human–dominated" landscapes. At least two approaches may be taken in the study of landscape ecology. The biocentric approach emphasizes the significance of landscape phenomena, and processes are assessed with reference to plant and animal communities (i.e., humans are incidental parts of the system). The anthropocentric approach places emphasis on human relationships within landscapes. Under the latter approach, short–term as well as long–term needs of humans are emphasized, along with the responsibilities of humans for the landscape and all its organisms. For example, the protection and conservation of natural ecosystems through nature reserves is seen as a specific kind of land use, reflecting not only human needs but also human responsibilities. Vink (1983) pointed out that urban land use has often been neglected in ecological studies. In Vink's view, "Towns and cities ought to be viewed as cultural ecosystems and urban ecology may be able to make important contributions to providing man with a better urban environment in the future."

Implementation of conservation programs and strategies in urban and urbanizing areas is only beginning, and the value of such work is becoming more widely recognized. Murphy (1988), in discussing the importance of maintaining biological diversity, pointed out that, "Our urban centers can be viewed as bellwethers of our global environmental fate. Our success at meeting the challenges of protecting biological diversity in urban areas is a good measure of our commitment to protect functioning ecosystems worldwide. If we cannot act as responsible stewards in our own backyards, the long–term prospects for biological diversity in the rest of this planet are grim indeed."

2

SOME EFFECTS OF URBANIZATION ON WILDLIFE AND WILDLIFE HABITAT

It is not our intent, in this chapter, to discuss in detail the known effects of urbanization on wildlife. Rather, we provide a brief overview as background to the more comprehensive discussion of corridors and reserves that follows in Chapter 3.

Urban development fragments natural habitats into smaller and more isolated units. In the process, it destroys habitat of many species, modifies habitat of others, and creates new habitat for some species (Fig. 1). Most metropolitan complexes can be characterized by three zones: (1) metropolitan centers, (2) suburbia, and (3) the rural–urban interface (VanDruff 1979). The metropolitan center, i.e., the inner city or downtown area, is highly modified and typically contains few wildlife species and little wildlife habitat. Starlings, pigeons, house sparrows, and a few other species may be common, although small–scale opportunities for habitat enhancement can increase species diversity. (Please see Appendix A for scientific names of plants and animals mentioned in the text.)

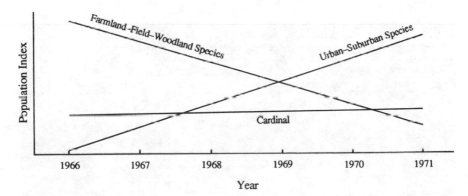

Fig. 1. Changes in breeding bird populations during early development of Columbia, Maryland, based on data of Geis (1974). See text (Aldrich and Coffin 1980) for a similar example.

Suburban areas are less densely developed than the city center and consequently possess more open space, e.g., backyards, community parks, cemeteries, and open land associated with industrial or business parks, and with schools, churches, hospitals, and other institutions. A greater diversity of wildlife may be found here, depending on how the various areas are managed.

The rural–urban interface zone offers the greatest opportunity for thoughtful planning to consider wildlife in the development process. Areas of natural habitat can still be preserved here and, consequently, more wildlife species are present.

Other features that characterize most urban areas were summarized by Leedy and Adams (1986) as follows:

- Buildings, streets, roads, parking lots, and other artificial constructions occupy much of the ground surface and form a largely impermeable and sterile covering of the soil which probably once supported native vegetation or cultivated crops.
- Runoff from paved areas is higher and more rapid with little infiltration to the underlying strata, which means a reduced rate of recharging of natural groundwater reservoirs and a lowering of the water table.
- Reduction in groundwater results in increased variation in natural stream flows.
- Runoff, particularly the first surges following a storm, may contain pollutants and toxic materials stemming from the urbanized area.
- Runoff from new construction in urban areas carries much more sediment per unit of area to receiving waters than runoff from developed areas or even from agricultural areas.
- Rainfall often increases downwind in heavily urbanized and industrialized areas.

Photo: J. Atkin

The inner city or downtown area of metropolitan complexes typically has little natural vegetation. Most opportunities for wildlife enhancement here relate to small–scale redevelopment sites and street–side plantings, corner plazas, terraces, balconies, and rooftop and window gardens. (Photo from National Geographic WORLD, © 1988 National Geographic Society, with permission.)

- The urban cores of large cities are generally warmer than the outer suburbs or surrounding countryside.
- Air and noise pollution often is considerably greater in urban as compared with surrounding areas.
- Except for well–tended, heavily fertilized and mulched lawn and garden areas, urban soils are likely to be modified detrimentally by mixtures of bricks and other building materials, and by compaction and loss of topsoil.
- Urban development often results in a loss of wildlife species considered specialists, and an increase of species considered generalists.
- Urban areas generally have fewer species of wildlife but a greater total animal biomass than nonurban areas.

The major focus of the present report relates most directly to the last two effects listed above, which are based on a number of research studies (Batten 1972, Walcott 1974, Aldrich and Coffin 1980, Beissinger and Osborne 1982, and Bezzel 1985, among others). For example, Aldrich and Coffin (1980) compared breeding bird use of a 38.5–ha mature eastern deciduous forest tract in Fairfax County, Virginia,

Photo: L.E. Dove

Suburban areas are less densely developed than the city center and consequently provide more open space. A greater diversity of wildlife may be found here, depending on how the various areas are managed.

in 1942, with bird use of the same tract in 1979 after it had become a well–established residential community (please see Appendix B for metric conversions to English units). Red–eyed vireos, ovenbirds, and scarlet tanagers were abundant in 1942 but were not found in 1979. In addition, the wood thrush was common in 1942 but only two territories were recorded in 1979. Other typical forest birds present in 1942 but lacking in 1979 were Acadian flycatcher, eastern wood pewee, yellow–throated vireo, worm–eating warbler, hooded warbler, and Louisiana waterthrush. However, gray catbirds, American robins, and house sparrows were numerous in 1979 but were absent in the area in 1942. Also more numerous in 1979 were blue jays, mockingbirds, starlings, cardinals, and song sparrows. The authors concluded that, with increased urbanization, "We may expect to have more Blue Jays, Mockingbirds, Gray Catbirds, American Robins, Cardinals and Song Sparrows, as well as Starlings and House Sparrows, but it will be at the expense of Wood Thrushes, Red–eyed Vireos, Ovenbirds, Scarlet Tanagers and other birds characteristic of the deciduous forests of eastern North America. *If we want both groups of species we must make certain that sufficiently large and undisturbed areas of the natural*

Photo: L.E. Dove

The rural–urban interface zone offers the greatest opportunity for thoughtful planning to consider wildlife in the development process. Areas of natural habitat can be more easily preserved in this zone and wildlife and other natural resource considerations, when initiated early in the planning stage, can result in lessened impact from development.

habitats are preserved to support the breeding of those specialized species that are dependent upon them." (emphasis added).

Other effects of urbanization on wildlife were summarized in a comprehensive annotated bibliography (Leedy 1979), and Adams (1988) reviewed some of the additional research since 1979. In addition, several recent symposia addressed, among other things, the effects of urbanization on wildlife (Stenberg and Shaw 1986, Johnson 1987, Adams and Leedy 1987).

How can the negative effects of development on wildlife and wildlife habitat be minimized through ecological landscape planning? The remaining chapters of this guidebook will address this question. The central planning theme is an integrated landscape approach of habitat reserves and interconnecting corridors. An equally important consideration is how areas are managed after development. Maintenance or enhancement of habitat quality (i.e., habitat management) is important and will affect the species of wildlife that will use a given area. For example, specific plant species, structural properties of the vegetation (e.g., amount of understory, etc.), and the number and distribution of snags will influence wildlife use, as will the successional stage of the vegetation and the interspersion of various habitat types. The amount and type of available water, supplemental food, and the distribution and kinds of gardens maintained by residents also will influence wildlife use. These, and other, management considerations are beyond the scope of the present report. Our focus, instead, is on pre–development planning and how such effort can be conducted to benefit wildlife and people.

3

URBAN WILDLIFE RESERVES AND CORRIDORS: THE STATE OF OUR UNDERSTANDING

Island biogeography theory has emerged as the conceptual focal point in the design of habitat corridors and reserves for wildlife. MacArthur and Wilson (1967) proposed the theory for oceanic islands and archipelagoes. Simply stated, they developed a model of island biogeography that explains the number of species inhabiting an island based on a dynamic equilibrium between immigration rates and extinction rates that are influenced in turn by island size (area) and isolation (distance) among islands and the mainland. In general, immigration rates are predicted to increase and extinction rates to decrease on larger, less isolated islands, resulting in a higher equilibrium number of species as compared to the number on smaller, more distant islands.

A number of investigators have studied application of the theory to terrestrial habitat "islands." Most research in this regard has dealt with documenting species–area relationships (Fig. 2), and little work has addressed the more difficult tasks of quantifying immigration and extinction rates. The review that follows focuses on such studies, both in urban and nonurban environments. A recurring observation is that habitat area (size) is a major factor accounting for differences in species richness (i.e., number of species).

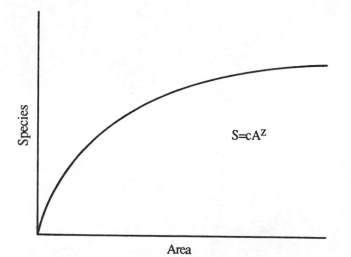

Fig. 2. A generalized relationship between species richness (number of species) and habitat area (size). S = species richness, A = habitat area, and c and z are constants. See text and Table 1 for specific examples.

Davis and Glick (1978) suggested that the application of island biogeography theory has considerable value in the study and strategy for conservation of urban ecosystems. They pointed out that the roles of most urban habitat islands have been little studied. Each city is a collection of habitat islands that may be considered either individually or collectively. The viability of these habitat islands as suitable wildlife habitat often depends on outside recruitment of animals, which is affected by the spatial arrangement of islands and the effectiveness of linkages of urban habitat patches with rural surroundings. These authors regarded small cities (and their associated habitat islands and corridors) as functionally similar to oceanic islands that are large and/or near to mainland habitat, with easy recruitment of wildlife species from the countryside through corridors that are short and effective. Large cities were regarded as functionally similar to small and/or distant oceanic islands, with inner-city islands separated from each other and from the rural matrix, and with corridors being less effective than those of small cities. The process of urbanization results in greater habitat fragmentation and disturbance, and increases the isolation of islands from one another and from the surrounding rural landscape, which typically brings about a reduction in species richness. A major conservation goal should be to design and implement conservation strategies to reduce the loss of species diversity.

The application of island biogeography theory to terrestrial urban habitats is international in scope. For example, Poynton and Roberts (1985) reviewed open space planning and management activities in Cape Town, Durban, and Johannesburg, South Africa, and the biogeographical literature dealing with habitat reserves and corridors. They pointed out that human amenity and recreational values have received much greater attention than biological considerations in planning and managing open space areas in these metropolitan environments. However, plans for the management and conservation of open spaces in Durban are still in an early stage of development and the University of Natal has initiated a biogeographically–oriented approach that may result in greater recognition of ecological considerations and in providing great amenity value to the community. Opportunities also exist in the other two cities for greater consideration of ecological factors. The authors concluded that ". . . the application of biogeographical principles to open space design provides the means for establishing ecologically resilient and diverse open space systems, which can combine low cost of maintenance with high scientific, educational, aesthetic and recreational potential."

In a related paper, Roberts and Poynton (1985) reported that it was common tendency to plan and manage open space areas centrally located in South African cities as highly manicured, parkland landscapes, favoring exotic plantings. Open space areas towards the periphery of cities were generally managed as natural areas. These authors argued that such an approach fosters a tendency to associate conservation with the rural landscape and to disassociate it from the urban environment. In their opinion, open space should be viewed as a multifunctional element within the urban landscape, important to conservation, public health, and spatial design, rather than merely a residential component needed to satisfy

A park or wooded open space area consisting of mature deciduous trees with a ground cover of closely cropped grass has far less value for wildlife than an area with mixed deciduous and evergreen species of different ages and multiple layers of vegetation. Dead trees, snags, or limbs provide desirable diversity. (From Leedy and Adams 1984)

demands of outdoor recreation. Natural habitat reconstruction and indigenous planting, both in more formal and in more derelict open space areas, would inexpensively meet aesthetic and amenity requirements, improve educational and scientific potential, and facilitate dispersal of native species throughout the urban environment.

WILDLIFE RESERVES IN THE METROPOLITAN LANDSCAPE

Vertebrates

Vizyová (1986) studied the importance of habitat area size, degree of habitat isolation (barrier effect), and percent vegetative cover on species number of land vertebrates in urban woodlots. Field work was conducted during 1982–1984 on 21 sites, ranging in size from 0.6 to 47 ha, in the town of Bratislava, Czechoslovakia. Study sites included city parks, cemeteries, and remnant woodlots within the town and surrounding suburbs. Species presence data were obtained by conducting censuses of visually and audibly observed animals (amphibians, reptiles, birds, and some mammals), and by small mammal trapping.

Habitat area (size) was the best predictor of the number of species of land vertebrates as a whole and of birds and amphibians separately. Species of mammals and reptiles correlated most closely with degree of habitat isolation. Independent variables determined most important in predicting total numbers of land vertebrate species (all classes combined) were: habitat area, degree of habitat isolation, and percentage of vegetative cover. These three variables accounted for 91% of the variation in species richness. Vizyová concluded that, for managing land vertebrate communities in urban woodlots, minimum island size should be at least 5 ha, but an optimum minimum area would be 20–30 ha. Smaller and more isolated woodlots should have denser vegetative cover. However, areas larger than 10 ha containing clearings will create conditions for some forest edge species. In other words, "in small areas the most effective factor increasing the species richness is dense vegetation in all layers, while in large habitat islands the species number may be increased also by a higher spatial heterogeneity."

Mammals, reptiles, and amphibians occupying habitat patches in the city of Oxford, England, were studied by Dickman (1987). Fifty isolated patches (0.16 to 20 ha in size) were studied during 1983 and 1984. They consisted of semi–natural and disturbed vegetation and most were located within the city limits of Oxford. Twenty mammalian species were recorded. More species were present in semi–natural habitats (woodland, long grass, scrub) than in intensively cultivated allotments. Five species of amphibians and four species of reptiles were recorded. Patch size and nearness to permanent water influenced amphibian and reptile use. For all vertebrate species studied, more species were usually retained in two small habitat patches than would be expected in a single larger patch equal to their combined area. For mammals, excluding large species such as fallow and roe deer, the author recommended that a system of small (≥ 0.65 ha) woodland habitat patches be maintained throughout the city area. Habitat patches (at least 0.55 ha in size) that provide permanent sources of water are important for retaining amphibians and reptiles.

Birds

Tilghman (1987a) studied the characteristics of urban woodlands affecting breeding bird diversity and abundance in Springfield, Massachusetts. Thirty-two woodlands, isolated by urban development and ranging in size from 1 to 69 ha, were studied during 1980 and 1981. For each woodlot, habitat size, isolation, vegetation characteristics, and human activity were determined.

Seventy–seven bird species were recorded, and woodland size was the most important variable affecting number of bird species observed (i.e., woodland size accounted for 79% of the variation in total species richness). Number of bird species increased rapidly as size of woodland increased from 1 to 25 ha. At 25 ha, about 75% of the maximum number of species were represented. Above 25 ha the increase in number of species with size was more gradual. Of 27 species more commonly found in larger woods, nine (broad–winged hawk, brown creeper, veery, brown thrasher, black–and–white warbler, chestnut–sided warbler, black–throated green

Photo: L.E. Dove

Urban woodlots provide habitat for a wide diversity of wildlife species.

warbler, ovenbird, and Canada warbler) were never observed in woods smaller than 5 ha. Eight species (particularly American robin, northern mockingbird, warbling vireo, and house sparrow) were most abundant in the smallest (1–5 ha) woodlots. The latter species are typical urban species usually found in residential or industrial habitats. Several species appeared to be insensitive to size of woodland (e.g., northern flicker, blue jay, and northern cardinal). In comparing her results with those of DeGraaf and Wentworth (1981), who reported on birds of urban and suburban residential areas of Springfield, Tilghman concluded that *urban woodlands* in her study had about 50% more bird species than *suburban residential areas* and about four times as many species as *urban residential areas*.

In addition to size of woodland, the number of adjacent buildings, density of the shrub layer, and proximity of trails (a measure of human activity) were significant in influencing bird species numbers, but much less so than size of woodland. Woods with streams flowing through them, or those adjacent to lakes, had greater bird species diversity and total bird abundance. Isolation of woodlots from larger woodland tracts (4–11 km away) had no apparent effect on species diversity and Tilghman hypothesized that the degree of isolation was probably negligible, relative to the dispersal ability of birds.

In a related paper, Tilghman (1987b) reported on characteristics of urban woodlands affecting winter bird diversity and abundance in Springfield. Forty–six bird species were recorded and, again, woodland size was the most important single variable affecting number of bird species observed (i.e., woodland size accounted for 21–36% of the variation in total species richness). Thus, winter birds appeared to be less sensitive to island size than did breeding birds. However, according to Tilghman, "certain winter birds, such as red–tailed hawks, ruffed grouse, winter wrens, white–winged crossbills, and pine siskins, will probably not be found in urban areas unless a few large woodlands are available."

Other variables significantly influencing winter birds were density of adjacent buildings, amount of edge, and distance to the nearest body of water. In comparing her results with those of DeGraaf and Wentworth (1981), Tilghman concluded that *urban woodlands* in her study had about 50% more bird species in winter than *suburban residential areas* (similar to breeding season data) and about twice as many species as *urban residential areas* (compared to four times as many during the breeding season). Smaller urban woodlands generally had winter bird species lists similar to those of urban residential habitats, whereas larger urban woodlands more nearly resembled other forested habitats in the Northeast with regard to species richness (similar to observations during the breeding season).

Table 1. Predicted numbers of species for urban terrestrial "habitat islands" of different sizes. See text for details.

Island size (ha)	Woodland birds[a]	Woodland birds[b]	Woodland birds[c]	Chaparral birds[d]	Land vertebrates[c]	Urban parks[e]	
						Flies	Beetles
1	---	---	6.4	1.6	8.7	---	---
2	---	24.0	13.8	2.5	13.5	---	---
4	13.0	27.0	21.2	3.4	21.0	25.2	6.6
8	21.0	31.0	28.6	4.3	32.8	29.7	7.7
12	27.0	33.0	32.9	4.8	42.5	32.6	8.5
16	29.0	36.0	36.0	5.2	51.1	34.9	9.0
20	31.0	37.0	38.3	5.5	58.9	36.8	9.5
24	31.5	39.0	40.3	5.7	66.2	38.4	9.9
30	32.5	40.0	42.7	6.0	76.4	40.5	10.4
36	33.0	42.0	44.6	6.2	85.8	42.2	10.8
42	33.5	43.0	46.2	6.4	94.7	43.8	11.2
65	---	48.0	---	7.0	---	48.5	12.3
100	---	---	---	7.5	---	53.7	13.6
200	---	---	---	---	---	63.2	15.8
300	---	---	---	---	---	69.5	17.3

[a] Estimated from Fig. 2 of Luniak (1983).
[b] Estimated from Fig. 2 of Tilghman (1987a).
[c] From Vizyová (1986).
[d] From Soulé *et al.* (1988).
[e] From Faeth and Kane (1978).

Urban woodlot size also was determined important for maintaining bird species diversity in Delaware (Linehan *et al.* 1967). These investigators studied breeding bird use of nine urban woodlots in northern Delaware during 1966 and 1967. Woodlots ranged in size from 0.8 to 14.4 ha. According to these authors: "Urban woodlots play a unique role in providing the habitats for many of the birds that are seen and enjoyed by residents of suburban areas throughout many of our densely settled sections. The diversity of bird life, unconsciously sought by most bird viewers, is largely dependent on the presence and the quality of woodlots in an urban area. Very dense populations of a large variety of breeding birds are found in urban woodlots of 20 or more acres [≥ 8.1 ha] which have adequate shrub understory, mature and dead standing trees, and vegetative edge types that are of sufficient width and proper quality." However, Whitcomb *et al.* (1981) pointed out that *area–sensitive* forest interior species were rare or absent in the Delaware study. (See the section "Wildlife Reserves in Other Than Metropolitan Landscapes" in this report for further discussion of area–sensitive species.)

Supporting evidence of the importance of habitat size to maintaining bird species diversity in urban forested areas is available from the U.S. Pacific Northwest (Gavareski 1976). This investigator studied some of the effects of vegetation modification and size of urban parks on bird populations in Seattle, Washington. Six forested urban parks and one natural area (a 61–ha forested tract outside of urban influence selected for comparative purposes) were studied during the 1971 breeding season. Parks were classified as follows: (1) native forest with little or no altered vegetation; (2) parkland where major expanses of forest undergrowth and trees were replaced with lawns, garden shrubbery, and trees; and (3) parkland where all subordinate vegetation was cleared, leaving only grass and trees. Two parks of each type—one large (> 40 ha) and one small (< 4 ha)—were studied. Major findings were:

1. The large forested park with a natural diversity of native vegetation was similar to the rural natural area with regard to number of bird species.

2. Numbers and diversity of bird species declined as modification of vegetation increased and park size decreased.

3. In each size group, species numbers differed most between the forested park with native vegetation and the two parks with modified vegetation.

4. Within each vegetation type, the large park had more species than the smaller park.

5. Typical urban species made up a larger percentage of the species composition in smaller and more modified parks.

The author concluded that "a diverse avifauna characteristic of Pacific Northwest lowland forests can be supported in urban areas as long as large park areas with native forest vegetation are maintained."

Most of the research to date concerning wildlife use of urban terrestrial habitat islands relates to forested tracts. However, a recent study (Soulé *et al.* 1988) documented bird use of chaparral, i.e., Mediterranean–type scrub habitat, in

California. These investigators studied 37 isolated fragments of canyon habitat, ranging in size from 0.4 to 104 ha, in coastal, urban San Diego County. Field work was conducted November 1985 to June 1986, and from September 1986 to February 1987. The researchers documented some of the effects of fragmentation and isolation of canyon habitats on native chaparral–requiring birds and presented evidence that species diversity in isolated canyons has been reduced over time. Independent variables determined to be most important in predicting species richness (in order of significance) were: canyon "age" (i.e., time since isolation of the habitat fragment by development), amount of total area consisting of chaparral, total area of canyon, and a fox–coyote variable. These four variables accounted for 90% of the variation in species richness. The fox–coyote variable represented the interactions among coyotes, foxes, and domestic cats, and the impact of those predators on chaparral–requiring birds. Absence of coyotes apparently resulted in higher numbers of gray foxes, domestic cats, and other avian predators, which increased predation on birds. The authors suggested that coyotes normally help to control the smaller predators, thus indirectly contribute to the maintenance of native, chaparral avifauna diversity.

Chaparral–requiring birds are relatively sedentary species. Therefore, Soulé and his co–workers argued that connectivity of habitat patches is probably an important landscape feature for maintaining diversity of these native species. They pointed out the lack of research in this area, but based on their own observations suggested that "most, if not all, of the chaparral–requiring species can use relatively narrow strips of vegetation." For example, they observed wrentits and rufous–sided towhees using strips as narrow as 1 m; and California quail, California thrashers, and Bewick's wren in strips less than 10 m in width. The authors concluded that "The most effective tool for the prevention of extinction of chaparral–requiring species in an urban landscape is the prevention of fragmentation in the first place by proper planning of urban and suburban development. Corridors of natural habitat, even quite narrow ones, are probably very effective in permitting dispersal between patches, thereby preventing or minimizing faunal collapse."

Mammals

Matthiae and Stearns (1981) studied mammalian species–area relationships and the effect of the surrounding landscape on species richness of forested habitat patches in southeastern Wisconsin. The study was conducted in the Milwaukee metropolitan area on southern mesic forest islands (beech–maple) ranging from 0.4 to 40 ha. The 22 forested patches were isolated by urban and agricultural landscapes. Only mammals readily live–trapped or otherwise observed (total of 13 species) were included in the study. No attempt was made to trap shrews, moles, weasels, or bats. In addition, the investigators pointed out that some species, including woodland bison, moose, wolverine, black bear, elk, and lynx had previously been extirpated from the region.

Species richness, with some variability, generally increased with island size. Rural sites were most diverse. Urban islands served as refuges for small rodents and larger nocturnal scavengers and omnivores (most notably gray squirrels and raccoons). Islands in the urban–rural transition zone had lower species richness and abundance. The authors speculated that this observation may have resulted from greater isolation of islands and the absence of diverse adjacent habitat in the area.

Invertebrates

Species richness and population densities of Diptera (flies) and Coleoptera (beetles) were studied by Faeth and Kane (1978) in nine city parks in Cincinnati, Ohio. Each park was a forested, or partially forested, island–like area surrounded by urban development, and ranged in size from 4.3 to 334.3 ha. Numbers of species of both Diptera and Coleoptera increased with area in a manner predicted by island biogeography theory. Although not addressed in this study, one might wonder whether increasing richness of insects influences the richness of insectivorous birds in such areas.

Vegetation Changes in Urban Reserves

Levenson (1981) examined the applicability of the concepts of island biogeography to the woody vegetation of parks and woodlots in metropolitan Milwaukee, Wisconsin. Forty–three woodlots, ranging from 0.03 to 40 ha, were investigated May–October 1975. Levenson found that species richness of woody vegetation was largely a function of natural and human–induced disturbance. Heavy human usage maintained "a continual state of disturbance resulting in an increased edge effect and a high species richness from colonization of less tolerant species." Woodlots less than 2.3 ha were classified as edge communities because of the many shade intolerant species present. Species richness generally increased with island size to about 2.3 ha as a result of a mix of intolerant and residual shade tolerant species. Larger islands showed a general decline in species richness up to a size of 3.8 ha due to loss of intolerant species and establishment of only shade tolerant species. "Species richness ceased to decline at approximately 3.8 ha, suggesting that only the shade–tolerant, mesophytic species remained." Thus, only by protecting large (> 4 ha), less disturbed woodlots can self-perpetuating examples of the southern mesic (beech–maple) forest type be maintained. However, Levenson concluded that smaller islands and fencerows also are of value because they maintain a mix of exotic, pioneer, and terminal plant community components and can function as "stepping stones" between larger forested areas.

Investigation of the groundlayer vegetation on the above study sites was reported by Hoehne (1981). She too found that disturbance, which affected species presence, density, and frequency, appeared to be the most influential factor regulating composition of the groundlayer vegetation. Species intolerant of trampling or compaction disappeared while others increased. The number of species present decreased from 25–60% between 1951 and 1975. Many native, herbaceous species, including bracted orchid and ferns (American maidenhair fern and Virginia grape–fern), decreased. Forested stands receiving moderately heavy human use had a greater diversity resulting from additional exotic and weedy species, than did lightly used stands. The author suggested that certain wooded islands could be reserved "as natural areas with limited use where the native flora might survive. Other areas could be established for heavier recreational use. *In this way the two objectives, preservation and recreation, could both be satisfied."* (emphasis added).

WILDLIFE RESERVES IN OTHER THAN METROPOLITAN LANDSCAPES

Bond (1957) was perhaps the first researcher to report that many species of small songbirds are dependent on relatively large forest tracts during the breeding season. Since that time, a number of investigators have studied the effects of forest fragmentation on these *area–sensitive* species. Based on a review of the literature, O'Meara (1984) recognized two basic groups of birds. Group 1 birds are restricted by minimum territory size. For small "islands" (< 10 ha), species occurrence is primarily a function of territory size, with species colonizing islands that meet their minimum territory size requirements. These tend to be edge species, permanent residents, or short–distance migrants that are granivorous or omnivorous in their feeding habits. Birds restricted to larger islands (> 10 ha) because of minimum territory requirements are mostly non–passerines and carnivorous. Group 2 birds are area–sensitive. Species in this group, primarily neotropical migrants, apparently are not limited by territory size requirements, but occur only in larger areas of contiguous forest. They may require forested areas 30 to > 100 ha in size, areas much greater than their minimum territory sizes. Birds in this group tend to be insectivorous in feeding habits. Following is a brief review of the empirical evidence.

Galli *et al.* (1976) studied bird use of forested habitat patches surrounded by open fields in central New Jersey. Ten size classes of mixed oak habitat islands were studied, ranging from 0.01 to 24.0 ha. Bird species richness (number of species) increased significantly through an island size of 24 ha. Habitat island size accounted for 85% of the variation in total species richness. Numbers of herbivores and omnivores were little influenced by island size (i.e., were size independent). Of the 46 total species recorded, 17 were found over the entire range of forest sizes greater than 0.01 ha, and these 17 species were considered size independent. Eighteen species were considered size dependent. Carnivores, including insectivores, were mostly size dependent and the increase in species richness above an island size of 1.5–2.0 ha was due almost entirely to an increase in insect–eating carnivores. The red–shouldered hawk was the only vertebrate predator recorded in the study and required a minimum area of 10 ha. Foliage height diversity did not change significantly with habitat island size, so the authors concluded that observed changes in species richness were due to island size. Robbins (1979) and Whitcomb *et al.* (1981) pointed out that, because the largest plot was only 24 ha, those species that are most critically dependent on area were lacking from all plots and consequently were not recognized as being area dependent. Absent were *Empidonax* flycatchers, blue–gray gnatcatcher, yellow–throated vireo, worm–eating warbler, and hooded warbler. These investigators speculated that the area may have already experienced extirpations of these "forest interior" species.

Research concerning long–term shifts in the composition of bird communities in relation to the size and degree of isolation of forest patches, and the level of human–related disturbance to such areas, was reviewed by Lynch and Whitcomb (1978). These investigators pointed out that there is no consensus on the relative importance of these three factors as determinants of avifaunal diversity, species composition, and turnover, and that it is difficult to separate disturbance phenomena as a group from size and isolation. However, the evidence is strong that small forested tracts fail as meaningful reserves for the forest–interior avifauna of eastern North America because large forested tracts are not experiencing the same drastic loss of species and individuals observed in smaller tracts. In the opinion of Lynch and Whitcomb, "Existing urban and suburban parks are unsuccessful as avifaunal reserves, probably as a result of their combination of small size, increasing isolation from sources of potential colonists, and high level of human–related disturbance."

In addition to reviewing the published literature dealing with area–sensitive forest bird species, Robbins (1979) also presented new data from his own continuing studies. He pointed out that a pattern has emerged from these studies. Area–sensitive species are predominantly long–distance insectivorous migrants that winter primarily in the New World tropics (e.g., flycatchers, vireos, and wood warblers). Conversely, short–distance migrants that have adapted to survival in edge habitats (e.g., jays, house wrens, catbirds, robins, starlings, blackbirds, and towhees), and permanent resident species, tend to maintain their populations despite urban development and associated forest fragmentation.

Supporting evidence for the pattern mentioned above was provided by Whitcomb *et al.* (1981). These investigators studied the relationship between insularity of patches of eastern deciduous forest and species composition of forest–associated breeding bird communities. Field work was conducted on 25 upland forest (oak–hickory) "islands" in central Maryland during 1974 and 1975. Forested patches ranged in size from 1.1 to 283 ha. Five additional point surveys were conducted in extensive woodlands (283–905 ha) in the region. Species composition varied with island size according to the following: (1) a negative correlation existed between number of edge species and island size, (2) a positive correlation existed between number of forest–interior species and island size, and (3) no relationship was observed between number of ubiquitous species and island size (Fig. 3).

Although there was a marked change in species composition, there was no significant change in overall species richness with island size. Edge species included gray catbird, brown thrasher, common yellowthroat, yellow–breasted chat, and indigo bunting. Included among the forest–interior species were black–and–white warbler, worm–eating warbler, ovenbird, Kentucky warbler, and hooded warbler. Ubiquitous species included cardinal, Carolina wren, Carolina

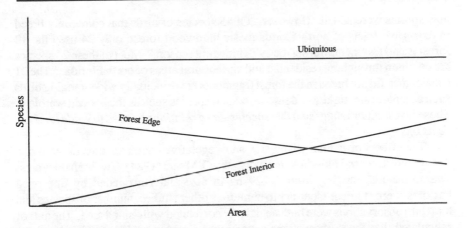

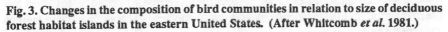

Fig. 3. Changes in the composition of bird communities in relation to size of deciduous forest habitat islands in the eastern United States. (After Whitcomb *et al.* 1981.)

chickadee, tufted titmouse, and blue jay. About 19 of the 93 species that comprised the regional pool of forest species were considered area–sensitive. These were primarily long–distance neotropical migrants that require relatively large interior forest habitat for breeding. These forest interior species were rare on small (1–5 ha) forest islands, more common on fragments of intermediate (6–14 ha) size, and most abundant on large (70+ ha) forested tracts. According to these authors, *continued reduction and isolation of forested lands will further reduce populations of these species.*

From studies in three different regions of the United States, Anderson and Robbins (1981) reported that frequency of occurrence of most bird species was highly correlated with forest size. Sixty–seven percent, 51%, and 73% of the species recorded were correlated with forest size in Maryland, Michigan, and Oregon, respectively. From studies in western Maryland, these investigators found that most long–distance neotropical migrants were observed least frequently in the smallest woodlots. Short–distance migrants (typical "edge" species) were found with increasing frequency as woodlot size decreased. Permanent residents did not show a consistent trend in either direction and most were found in good numbers in isolated woodlots of all sizes.

Two Florida studies add to our knowledge base of the effects of forest fragmentation on breeding birds. Harris and Wallace (1984) investigated the relationship between bird species richness and size of 12 mesic hardwood forest stands in the north–central portion of the state. Study sites ranged from 0.4 to 30.0 ha in size. Habitat island size accounted for 79% of the variation in species richness. A doubling of the number of species was noted for every 7.25–fold increase in island size. The authors reported that species seemed to colonize islands in a regular, orderly fashion. Similar–sized islands had the same complement of species present. As island size increased, the species included on smaller islands were retained and new species were added. However, "Of 45 species of birds that commonly breed in expansive tracts of north Florida mesic hardwood forest, only 24 used the 12 forest island fragments during the 1978 breeding season." Most of these 24 species are common throughout residential and agricultural areas of north Florida. "The 21 species that did not breed in the forest fragments are principally wide–ranging birds such as raptors and turkey or dense woodland species such as the hooded warbler." These investigators suggested that *species–area relations be used to guide land use decisions.*

The effects of habitat island size and vegetative characteristics on an avian community in central Florida were reported by O'Meara (1984). Twelve baldcypress swamp islands, ranging from 7–229 ha in size and surrounded by improved pastures, were studied. Contrary to numerous other studies, number of species and total bird observations were both negatively correlated with island area. The author speculated that these obsevations apparently were due to "edge effect" and the paucity of forest–interior, neotropical migrant species. (The value of edge habitat in creating habitat diversity, thus wildlife diversity, is well documented.) O'Meara concluded that "Forest fragmentation may affect breeding–season communities differently in different regions as a result of species distribution limits, especially neotropical migrant species." For example, in the U.S., southeastern states typically have lower breeding bird diversities than more northerly states, due largely to the greater diversity of neotropical migrants (area–sensitive species) in northern latitudes. O'Meara concluded that, in central Florida, baldcypress ponds 10 to 20 ha in size retained the complement of breeding season bird species using this vegetation type.

Research reviewed to this point has dealt with breeding birds. The question of whether or not migrating birds use isolated woodlots smaller than those required during the breeding season was addressed by Blake (1986). Fourteen woodlots, ranging in size from 1.8 to 600 ha and surrounded by nonforest habitat, were studied in east–central Illinois during spring (1979–1981) and fall (1979–1980) migrating periods. Woodlot size accounted for 72% of the variation in species number. Although larger woodlots accumulated a greater total number of species, Blake concluded that even small tracts may be used temporarily by a wide variety of species and the presence of even small patches of natural habitat may increase the ability of migrants to pass successfully over highly disturbed landscapes. However, in citing Graber and Graber (1983), Blake cautioned that small woodlots may not be sufficient as refuges for migrants if larger blocks of forest are not available also. For example, according to the Grabers, spring warblers were able to accumulate fat when foraging in southern Illinois where total forest cover is extensive, but experienced a net energy loss while foraging in isolated woodlots in east–central Illinois.

In comparing data from his study with breeding season data (Blake and Karr 1984), Blake observed greater species richness during migration than during the breeding season. He attributed these observations to (1) arrival of transient species during migration that do not breed in the region, and (2) occurrence of species in woodlots smaller than those typically required for breeding. For example, during migration many long–distance migrants, like the ovenbird and other warblers, occurred in a wider size range of woodlots than during the breeding season. Also, several permanent residents, like the black–capped chickadee, tufted titmouse, and white–breasted nuthatch, were observed in smaller woodlots during the migration seasons than during the breeding season. Higher nest predation and parasitism, increased competition, and other factors operating in small woodlots during the breeding season may have influenced these observations.

URBAN WETLAND RESERVES

Water is a vital natural resource—a requirement for both wildlife *and* human life. It is probably fair to say that we are still not managing it wisely. For example, many aquifers continue to be depleted and not adequately recharged, and various water bodies are still used as common dumping grounds for numerous by–products of present–day society. In financial terminology, water might best be considered a capital asset, and capital depletion is an unsound business practice. Yet, with respect to water, that is what has been done in the past, and to a lesser extent, is continuing today.

Wetlands are an important part of this capital asset. Estimates indicate that the United States had about 87 million ha of wetlands at the time of colonial settlement. Less than half that amount remains today. Between the mid–1950's and the mid–1970's, annual wetland losses averaged 185,490 ha (Tiner 1984). Agricultural development involving drainage was responsible for 87% of those losses, while urban and other development caused 8% and 5% of the losses, respectively.

Two wetland types– –inland flats and ponds– –showed gains between the mid–1950's and mid–1970's (Tiner 1984). Pond acreage nearly doubled from 931,000 ha to 1.8 million ha, primarily due to farm pond construction in the central and Mississippi flyways. Most of the pond acreage came from former uplands, although 58,725 ha of forested wetlands and 155,925 ha of emergent wetlands were changed to open water.

Contributing to past wetland losses was a perception on the part of many people that wetlands were nothing more than wastelands with little or no practical value. Some still hold that view today. This is unfortunate because wetlands provide many benefits. We know that they are among the most productive habitats for wildlife. They help to control floods and erosion, purify water, recharge groundwater supplies, and they have recreational and aesthetic values.

A good example of an urban wetland reserve serving multiple functions is Tinicum Marsh, near Philadelphia, Pennsylvania. The marsh lies within the Tinicum National Environmental Center, which is managed by the U.S. Fish and Wildlife Service. The area provides habitat for a variety of wildlife species. More than 280 bird species have been recorded there, and Tinicum is the only Pennsylvania location of the eastern mud turtle and one of only three places in the state

U.S. Fish and Wildlife Service

Tinicum Marsh, near Philadelphia, Pennsylvania, provides valuable wildlife habitat, functions to improve water quality, and offers high quality programs in environmental education and wildlife-oriented recreation through the Tinicum National Environmental Center.

where the large red–bellied turtle is found——both of these species are on the state endangered species list (Hester 1985).

Tinicum also functions to improve water quality. Three sewage treatment plants discharge treated sewage into the marsh. On a daily basis, the marsh removes 7.0 metric tons of BOD, 4.4 metric tons of phosphorus, 3.9 metric tons of ammonia, and 62.6 kg of nitrate, while adding 18.2 metric tons of oxygen to the water (Grant and Patrick 1970 as cited in Tiner 1984).

In addition to the above functions, Tinicum National Environmental Center provides high quality programs in environmental education and wildlife–oriented recreation.

The potential for creating man–made urban wetlands for stormwater control and wildlife enhancement was studied by Bascietto and Adams (1983), Adams *et al.* (1985a, b), and Duffield (1986). Research in Columbia, Maryland indicated that, per hectare, mallard breeding pair use of shallow ponds (average size 0.2 ha, average depth 0.7 m, with gently sloped sides) was about 2.4 times greater than use of deep ponds (average size 0.3 ha, average depth 2.1 m, with steep side slopes), and about 3.2 times greater than use of lakes (average size 12.1 ha, average depth 3.7 m). Mallard broods also preferred shallow ponds to deep ponds and lakes.

Greater use of shallow ponds in Columbia also was noted for a variety of other wetland birds. In addition to waterfowl and related species, other wetland birds recorded using permanent–water impoundments were: great blue heron; green–backed heron; killdeer; common snipe; spotted, solitary, and least sandpipers; yellowlegs; and red–winged blackbirds. During migration, these species preferred shallow ponds to deep ponds by more than three to one. Shallow ponds were preferred to lakes by more than 46 to one. A similar preference was shown for shallow ponds during the breeding season.

Lakes in Columbia were most attractive to waterfowl during the migratory and wintering seasons. In addition to the mallard, a variety of other species (16 recorded) also used the lakes as resting and feeding sites during these time periods. Most notable of the species wintering in the area, or those using the lakes as stop–over sites during migration, were Canada goose, blue–winged teal, ring–necked duck, canvasback, and lesser scaup.

The attitudes of Columbia, Maryland residents toward urban impoundments were reported by Adams *et al.* (1984). Ninety–eight percent of the respondents said they enjoy viewing birds and other wildlife that make use of the city's impoundments and 94% agreed that it would be desirable to design and manage future stormwater–control basins for fish and wildlife, as well as for flood and sediment control if this was feasible from technical and economic standpoints. Seventy–five percent of the respondents felt that permanent bodies of water added to real estate values, and 73% said that they would pay more for property located in a neighbor-

Photo: L.W. Adams

Man–made wetlands can be designed for stormwater control and wildlife enhancement in the urban environment.

hood with stormwater control basins designed to enhance fish or wildlife use. Although residents had some concerns about nuisances, hazards, and maintenance of these structures, they considered benefits to outweigh undesirable features.

WILDLIFE CORRIDORS

Increased research activity over the past two decades has focused on planning and management of various man–made corridors. In the United States, four symposia on environmental concerns in rights–of–way (ROW) management were convened (Tillman 1976, 1981; Crabtree 1984; Byrnes and Holt 1987), and increased attention has been devoted to highway corridors (Leedy 1975, Leedy *et al.* 1975, Adams and Geis 1981, Leedy and Adams 1982, among others). Many studies have dealt with corridor planning (e.g., routing to minimize impact), and various management approaches to enhance conditions for wildlife. ROW habitats comprise significant acreages and improved management of these areas can benefit many wildlife species (see Leedy *et al.* 1980 for examples relating to the electric utility industry). In addition, fencerows (Best 1983, Shalaway 1985, among others) and shelterbelts (Martin 1978; Podoll 1979; Cassel and Wiehe 1980; Emmerich and Vohs 1982; Yahner 1982 a,b; Yahner 1983 a,b) can benefit wildlife.

We know that these various man–made corridors, depending upon width, habitat type and structure, nature of surrounding habitat, human use patterns, and perhaps other factors, can serve as useful habitat in their own right, can fragment existing habitats, or can serve as travel lanes for seasonal movements of wildlife and as interconnecting links between or among larger habitat areas. The focus on corridors in this report is on the latter.

Wildlife Corridors in the Metropolitan Landscape

During the course of the present study, we found little empirical evidence documenting the use and value of interconnecting corridors among habitat reserves (islands). Similar conclusions were recently reached by Noss (1983), Simberloff and Cox (1987), and Soulé *et al.* (1988). Simberloff and Cox (1987) reported that corridors might alleviate threats from inbreeding depression and demographic stochasticity, assist in maintaining persistence of species requiring more resources than are available in single refuges, and they may constitute important habitat in their own right (e.g., riparian corridors). However, according to these authors, ". . . much of the current literature concerning corridors fails to consider potential disadvantages and often assumes potential benefits without the support of sufficient biological data, or even explicit recognition that such data are needed." For example, corridors may facilitate transmission of contagious diseases, fires, or other catastrophes; may increase exposure of animals to predators, domestic animals, and poachers; and the monetary costs of establishing and maintaining corridors might better be spent on other conservation measures. They concluded that decisions regarding corridors should ". . . be based on data or well–founded inference, not on overarching generalities."

In a reply to Simberloff and Cox (1987), Noss (1987a) argued the case for corridors in the human–dominated landscape. He pointed out that "Perhaps the best argument for corridors is that the original landscape was interconnected." Further, habitat connectivity declines with human modification of the landscape and the use of corridors is an attempt to maintain or to restore some of the natural landscape connectivity. Noss did not suggest that corridors be built between naturally isolated habitats. Soulé *et al.* (1988) also believed that the advantages of corridors outweigh any disadvantages, particularly in urban–suburban settings. We concur.

Noss (1987a) agreed with Simberloff and Cox (1987) that habitat corridors are currently popular in land use plans and conservation strategies, and that few experimental data are available to support or to refute their value. He stated, "No doubt more research is needed to develop optimal connectivity strategies, but the continuing severance of natural linkages in many landscapes suggests that active strategies to combat the process and the consequences of fragmentation must proceed quickly, with or without 'sufficient' data." Necessary widths of corridors will vary depending on habitat structure and quality within individual corridors, nature of the surrounding habitat, human use patterns, and particular species that are expected to use the corridor. For example, narrow fencerow corridors might suffice for many farmland species, but much wider corridors are necessary for wilderness species.

Noss suggested that biologists also should consider the anthropocentric functions of corridors, reserves, and other open spaces in developed landscapes. These quality–of–life factors (e.g., scenery, recreation, pollution abatement, and land value enhancement) are of considerable importance to landscape architects and planners. Biologists should work with these professionals to develop corridor designs that can optimize quality of both the human and nonhuman environment.

Pertinent in this regard is the call for a national "Greenways for Americans" initiative from the President's Commission on Americans Outdoors (Anonymous 1987, Salwasser 1987). Among other things, the Commission recommended a network of greenways across the United States and called for linking up existing parks, river and stream corridors, grasslands, hiking and biking trails, abandoned rail lines, and other areas of open space for use by people and wildlife. One of several stated goals was to "Link urban and rural areas into a diverse network for the dual purposes of recreation and conservation of natural resources" (Salwasser 1987). (See Forman and Godron 1986 for various human uses of corridors.)

Most natural areas are identified and established on the basis of content within the area (Noss 1987b). However, Noss argued that consideration also should be given to the context within which a natural area lies (i.e., consideration of the structure and use of the surrounding landscape). Such an approach addresses the importance of the total landscape mosaic. In practice, one should combine the use of corridors and various multiple use zoning strategies to form an integrated network of clustered reserves. He stated, "Those who plan and design reserve systems should evaluate riparian strips, coastal strips, ridge systems, powerline and highway rights–of–way, and other landscape features as potential corridors to functionally interconnect isolated natural areas."

With regard to riparian corridors, Budd *et al.* (1987) reviewed the literature and reported results of a case study to provide guidelines for determining optimal stream corridor widths in the Bear–Evans Creek watershed located in King County, Washington. The watershed is in a rural portion of the county on the eastern edge of metropolitan Seattle. King County is the most populated county in the Pacific Northwest and developmental pressure is continuing.

Budd and his co–workers outlined the benefits of stream corridors as including (1) aesthetic and recreational values, (2) preservation of water quality, (3) minimization of runoff impacts, (4) control of erosion, and (5) maintenance of fish and wildlife habitat. They evaluated the physical and biological conditions critical to sustaining stream ecosystems based on an analysis of stream corridor needs for fisheries and wildlife. Much of the research reviewed relative to wildlife habitat supported buffer widths of 30.5 m on each side of a stream. However, results from the Bear–Evans Creek watershed study indicated that a 15–m buffer width provided an adequate protection barrier for many reaches of the watershed. Under conditions of poor habitat, extremely severe bank slopes, and extensive wetland areas, practical corridor widths were variable.

Based on the above–mentioned literature review and case study, Cohen *et al.* (1987) proposed a county–wide set of uniform policies and regulations to maintain and protect stream corridor riparian habitat in King County, Washington. Stream classifications were based on Stream Types 1–5 of the State of Washington's Department of Natural Resources. Types 1–4 are natural, usually perennial, water courses and have significant influence on water quality downstream. They may

Wildlife corridors can help to maintain or restore some of the natural landscape connectivity. They are valuable to both people and wildlife.

include wetlands and lakes. Type 5 encompasses all other waters, perennial or intermittent, including seepage areas, ponds, and sinks. They may lack a well–defined channel and may have short periods of spring runoff.

Cohen and co–workers outlined eight recommendations for protecting stream corridors, two of which relate to buffer widths and are presented below.

1. ". . . new development adjacent to streams should preserve an undisturbed corridor of sufficient width to maintain the natural hydraulic and habitat functions of each stream. Water Types 1–4 should have a corridor not less than 15 m (50 ft) wide from the ordinary high–water mark on each side of the stream. Type 5 waters should have a corridor of not less than 7.6 m (25 ft) from the ordinary high–water mark. A greater width may be required for large urban developments, especially if runoff, pollutants, or other byproducts will impact this buffer.

2. ". . . slopes over 40% and wetlands defined by King County which are adjacent to streams should be included within all stream corridors. Where wetlands or steep slopes extend beyond the above 15–m (50–ft) corridor based on ordinary high water, the corridor buffer should be expanded to include these features."

The authors pointed out that much of the research reviewed in their earlier publication (Budd *et al*. 1987) supported buffer widths of 30.5 m. However, based on their case study and "the political realities of imposing large buffer widths on areas facing development pressure," they believe their recommendations represent a workable compromise. They concluded ". . . we have tried to strike a compromise between the conservative recommendations of the scientific community and the minimal restrictions desired by developers, to create a workable and effective system of policies and guidelines. By informing developers and new landowners of the benefits of riparian ecosystem protection for real estate amenity, provision of open space and recreation, protection of fish and wildlife habitat, improved human habitation, and high–quality water source, a better environment can be created for community development and a valuable resource can be protected."

The lack of ecological knowledge of corridors in the metropolitan landscape is not confined to the United States. For example, Williams *et al*. (1987) surveyed the extent of surviving hedgerows in Kingsbury, now a suburban part of the Borough of Brent in northwest London, England. Based on historical records, they estimated that, at one time, there had been 80 km of hedgerow in Kingsbury. The authors estimated that about 14.5 km of hedgerow remain. There was a large loss of farmland and hedgerows between 1920–1940 corresponding to the rapid spread of suburbia in the vicinity of London. Williams and co–workers pointed out that few studies have been conducted on hedgerows in suburban areas and that the wildlife value of remnant hedgerows within such areas is not well documented.

Corridors in Other Than Metropolitan Landscapes

MacClintock *et al*. (1977) provided some evidence for the value of a habitat corridor between a small, 14.2–ha forest fragment and a larger, 162–ha woodland in maintaining the forest breeding bird community in the smaller tract. Open fields were present on three sides of the 14.2–ha forest fragment. The fourth side was connected to the 162–ha woodland by a narrow, disturbed corridor of about 6.1 ha, consisting of grazed woodland, early second growth, and a stream. The larger woodland, in turn, was connected by several corridors to a forested tract in excess of 4,000 ha.

Both the deciduous and coniferous portions of the forest fragment showed close similarity, in terms of breeding birds, to these two habitat types in the larger, 162–ha woodland. However, edge species recorded in the deciduous portion of the fragment, but not in the larger woodland, included gray catbird, indigo bunting, common yellowthroat, bobwhite, and yellow–breasted chat. Coniferous forest had 24 species in common. Those species most abundant in the surrounding larger pine woods also were the most common in the fragment. The authors stated, "Thus there is little evidence that the status of the Springfield East plot as part of a forest fragment resulted in avifaunal depletion."

The ovenbird, among the species least likely to colonize small tracts in the Maryland Piedmont, was the most abundant species in the large forested tract with a density of 254 males/100 ha, and a single territory was documented in the connecting corridor. The corridor also furnished breeding territory for several other forest interior species. The authors concluded that the upland forest fragment of 14.2 ha "was utilized as breeding habitat by most of the bird species which characterize the avifaunal communities of extensive upland eastern forests." The connecting corridor appeared to be quite important in that regard. However, limitations to the study were reported by Margules *et al*. (1982) and Simberloff and Cox (1987) who pointed out that it did not separate corridor effects from the effects of proximity of the habitat island to the extensive forest.

The importance of habitat patch connectivity to population survival of the white–footed mouse was investigated by Fahrig and Merriam (1985). The objectives of this study were to: "(1) develop a model of patch dynamics that can be applied to field data, and (2) test certain predictions of the model by field work to answer the question: does population survival within a patch depend on the degree to which it is isolated from other patches?" The model was applied to populations of the white–footed mouse in six deciduous woodlots in southeastern Ontario, Canada. Two of the woodlots (3.7 and 3.8 ha in size) were isolated by agricultural fields and the other four (1.5–9.8 ha) were connected by fencerows. The white–footed mouse was selected for testing the model for a number of reasons, including the fact that considerable local population data were available for the species (i.e., birth rates, death rates, dispersal rates, and density) as well as life history characteristics.

Based on reviews of several studies, the authors pointed out that: (1) the density of white–footed mouse populations in small isolated woodlots decreases with the distance between woodlot and a large forest, (2) autumn emigration significantly decreases mouse populations in small woodlots (< 3 ha) unless compensated by immigration, and (3) overwintering mortality in populations inhabiting small patches can cause local extinctions before spring. The model predicted that white–footed mouse populations in isolated woodlots have lower growth rates than those in connected woodlots, and this was verified by field results. The authors concluded that the combined effect of these factors is a higher probability of extinction in isolated habitat patches. (Wegner and Merriam 1979 also reported that forest birds and small mammals used fencerows between woodlots much more than they traveled across open fields.)

RESEARCH NEEDS

To date, little wildlife research effort has focused on the urban environment. A recent survey of North American colleges and universities found that 5% of wildlife research projects during the 1983–1984 school year was related to urban wildlife with about 2% of wildlife research budgets devoted to urban wildlife studies (Adams *et al.* 1987). Even so, this effort was greater than that in state and federal agencies reported by Lyons and Leedy (1984) and probably reflects to some degree the relatively recent emergence of urban wildlife as a new dimension in the wildlife profession. A good review of research needs regarding urban wildlife in general was provided by Progulske and Leedy (1986).

Our objective in this section is to briefly outline some of the needs, as we perceive them, relative to habitat reserves and corridors in the urban and urbanizing environment. In some (perhaps many) respects, practice is running ahead of research. Reserves and corridors are currently popular in landscape designs, but our knowledge with regard to both is limited.

Certainly a major constraining factor to our limited knowledge is a lack of research funding. Over 53% of the respondents to the survey reported by Adams *et al.* (1987) indicated that more urban wildlife–related research would be initiated if additional funds were available. Greater recognition and appreciation of the need for, and value of, such research might be helpful in this regard.

We noted in Chapter 1 that either a biocentric or anthropocentric approach could be taken in the study of "landscape ecology." The latter approach might be most appropriate in the urban and urbanizing environment. However, Adams *et al.* (1987) reported that only about 15% of the urban wildlife–related research of selected North American colleges and universities during the 1983–1984 school year dealt with human dimensions, planning, education, or economic aspects. In our opinion, these subject areas are particularly important in the urban environment and warrant greater attention.

Future establishment and management of urban wildlife reserves and corridors will, most likely, depend largely on public demand– –what people want and what they will support. Therefore, human–dimensions research seems quite important. For example, more research is needed on attitudes, perceptions, opinions, preferences, knowledge, and needs of the urban public with regard to wildlife. Also needed is better knowledge of how various urban open spaces are used by the public.

Photo: L.W. Adams

More research is needed on how various urban open spaces are used by the public.

Quantification of "quality–of–life" factors like scenery, recreation, pollution abatement, and land value enhancement is needed.

We have made some progress in this area in recent years. Limited research has documented considerable interest in wildlife by the urban public but a striking lack of knowledge about the resource (see Adams 1988 for a recent review). Therefore, more research of an educational nature would be useful. For example, research focusing on more effective approaches to conveying wildlife–related information to various public audiences might be initiated (see the session "Progress and Needs in Wildlife Resource Education" in McCabe 1988 for a good review). Finally, more research is needed on how to balance human use and enjoyment of urban wildlife reserves and corridors with wildlife use of the areas.

Research of a biological/ecological nature should not be neglected. For example, Shaffer (1981) felt that further work on habitat size relationships with birds would be useful, and that such work should be extended to nonavian species. Research on the relationship between percent of occupied habitat patches of various sizes and the potential longevity of the populations they support should be conducted. In other words, there is a need to know both the frequency with which species occur in habitat patches of different sizes, and the species–specific extinction/colonization rates typical of those units. Differences may result due to habitat quality as well as to habitat quantity. Shaffer believed that more research on the development of theoretical and simulation models of populations would be useful, as would further work on population genetics to obtain better knowledge of the breeding structure and genetic variability of particular species and the role of genetic variability in population growth and regulation. Our knowledge of "minimum viable populations" is limited.

With regard to mammal use of forested habitat patches, Matthiae and Stearns (1981) believed that further research was needed on effects of home range size, habitat connectivity, human disturbance, and adjacent varied habitats.

The individual importance of habitat patch size, its degree of isolation, and human–related disturbance to wildlife use of urban reserves and corridors needs clarification. Also, more research is needed in habitats other than forested ones as well as more work during the various seasons of the year.

Our knowledge of corridors serving as interconnecting links between and among habitat reserves is limited. Objective evaluation of advantages and/or disadvantages of such corridors should be undertaken (see the section "Wildlife Corridors in the Metropolitan Landscape" of this report and Simberloff and Cox 1987 for further discussion).

Riparian habitats (stream corridors) are of considerable current interest in the United States. More research is needed on the nature of wildlife species dependence upon riparian habitat to serve as a basis for resource planning and management (Budd *et al.* 1987). Included would be more work on minimal area and critical habitat necessary to support indigenous species. Budd and his co–workers also pointed out that, with regard to forested riparian habitat, the buffer width necessary to provide a natural supply of woody debris to a stream (to assist in maintaining stream structure) is unknown. However, most woody structure in streams is derived from within 31 m of the bank (Bottom *et al.* 1983 as cited in Budd *et al.* 1987).

The British countryside is widely known for its extensive network of hedgerows. However, Williams *et al.* (1987) pointed out that few studies have been conducted on hedgerows in suburban areas and that the wildlife value of remnant hedgerows within such areas is not well documented.

Consideration also should be given to vegetation of reserves and corridors as well as to wildlife. For example, with regard to woody vegetation in the Milwaukee, Wisconsin metropolitan area, Levenson (1981) recommended that top priority be given to research programs and management strategies for American beech and other species with specialized or low dispersal potential.

The monitoring and evaluation of specific design schemes *following* development, and the reporting of results to wildlife biologists, landscape architects, planners, and other professionals would be of great value. For example, research involving the general approach to landscape design for wildlife habitat proposed by Lyle (1987) and briefly outlined in Chapter 4 of this report would be helpful, as would empirical evaluation of innovative design schemes proposed by Goldstein *et al.* (1981, 1983). Under typical past practice, once the design has been approved, and the necessary permits obtained for a development site, little follow–through has documented how well the scheme works. Post–development monitoring and evaluation, to help separate good practices from bad ones, would be highly useful to planners, designers, developers, biologists, and regulatory authorities with regard to future development projects.

Finally, real estate in urban and urbanizing areas has high economic value. A few specific examples of approaches to providing wildlife reserves and corridors in such areas are presented in Chapter 5. Additional research on innovative approaches and methods for acquiring and managing open space lands for people and for wildlife conservation is needed.

4

GUIDELINES TO ECOLOGICAL LANDSCAPE PLANNING AND WILDLIFE CONSERVATION

In Chapter 3, we reviewed the present state of knowledge regarding habitat reserves and corridors in the urban environment. We noted that empirical evidence is available documenting the applicability of island biogeography theory to terrestrial habitat reserves and corridors, including those in urban areas.

Most research on the subject has dealt with birds. Consequently, we know more about the needs of birds than we do about the needs of other classes of wildlife. We know that even with no prior planning effort some species will be found in urban areas, and that these tend to be exotic species. Examples include starlings, pigeons, and house sparrows. However, with improved management of backyards, parks, cemeteries, community open spaces, and other areas, a variety of birds can be attracted if minimum territory size requirements are met along with other needs of food, water, and cover. For small areas (<10 ha), these tend to be habitat "generalists" (e.g., cardinals, jays, house wrens, catbirds, robins, etc.). Most are edge species, permanent residents, or short–distance migrants, and granivorous or omnivorous in feeding habits. For larger areas (>10 ha), if the above requirements are met, non–passerines may be added to the bird community. These tend to be carnivorous in feeding habits (e.g., hawks and owls).

Research also has found that some species of birds are *area–sensitive* and can be maintained only if relatively large tracts of natural habitat are retained. Area–sensitive, forest interior species may require forested areas of 30–100 ha. These species tend to be habitat "specialists" (e.g., many of the flycatchers, vireos, and wood warblers). Most are long–distance (neotropical) migrants and insectivorous in feeding habits. Habitat area (size) is the most significant factor accounting for differences in species richness in numerous studies conducted to date.

We noted that little research has been conducted on the value of corridors as interconnecting links among habitat reserves. However, a strong argument for such corridors is the fact that the original landscape was interconnected, and our efforts in this regard should be to maintain or restore some of the natural landscape connectivity. Needed widths of corridors will vary depending upon species of interest, habitat type and structure, nature of surrounding habitat (including topography), human use patterns, and perhaps other factors. Considerations also should extend to vegetation of reserves and corridors as well as to wildlife. For example, wooded corridors through agricultural land in Wisconsin may need to be slightly over 100 m wide to sustain beech trees and about 30 m wide to sustain sugar maple (Ranney *et al.* 1981).

A considerable literature base has developed on wildlife use of man–made corridors under various management schemes, e.g., highway and powerline rights–of–way, but most studies have not addressed the issue of habitat connectivity, i.e., corridors can fragment habitat (thus serve as barriers to wildlife movement) as well as serve as interconnecting links among habitat reserves.

Urban wetland reserves can serve multiple purposes. We know that wetlands are among the most productive habitats for wildlife. They help to control floods and erosion, purify water, recharge groundwater supplies, and they have recreational and aesthetic values. There is evidence that useful man–made wetlands can be created in connection with modern urban stormwater management practices.

The remainder of this chapter will focus on how the knowledge base, reviewed in Chapter 3 and briefly summarized above, can be applied to the development of conservation schemes for the urban and urbanizing environment.

A CONSERVATION STRATEGY

In the United States, there appears to be growing interest in wildlife conservation within both the landscape architecture profession and the planning profession. For example, in the opening session of a national symposium on urban wildlife, in November 1986, John Wacker, then President of the American Society of Landscape Architects (ASLA), stated: "In reviewing the nearly 40 national policies of the American Society of Landscape Architects, . . . I found that we have no policy on wildlife. Perhaps it is time for us to join with you, and I suggest this as a challenge to landscape architects, to begin to develop a policy on wildlife that will, especially in the urban focus, help us to work with you in a more cohesive way." (Wacker 1987).

In a follow–up on the above remarks, the Urban Wildlife Committee of The Wildlife Society was charged (in March 1987) to assist the ASLA in developing such a statement. The policy statement has been prepared, and is scheduled to be considered by ASLA in November 1988.

A general approach to landscape design for wildlife habitat was outlined by Lyle (1987). He stated:

> ". . . providing suitable conditions for plant and animal
> communities is a goal for every landscape everywhere,
> including urban, suburban, and rural landscapes, and a goal
> that should be seriously pursued at every level of environ–
> mental planning and design. Ideally, every regional plan,
> urban general plan, and design for a city park or a backyard
> should include specific provisions for wildlife habitat. To
> date, this has not been commonly done, except in some
> instances involving rare or endangered species. If planners
> and designers are to respond to this challenge, we need to
> establish some approaches and a broad, useful conceptual
> basis for planning and design for wildlife."

For landscape planning purposes, Lyle distinguished six fundamentally different habitat types, all differing in size, form, population potentials, and management practice. These were termed wild areas, wild patches, wild enclaves, corridors, exotic greens, and wildlife parks, the last four being highly applicable to urban areas. Lyle noted that categorizing habitat areas in this manner provides a coherent means of dealing with wildlife concerns at each scale of planning. He also cautioned that the approach was not yet advanced to the stage of a universally applicable planning tool and called for further applications in practice as well as more research on its utility.

Wildlife biologists should welcome the initiatives cited above and should endeavor to work more closely with planning and landscape architecture professionals to advance the conservation of wildlife and wildlife habitat in urban and developing areas.

How does one go about planning for urban wildlife? In our view, a broad conservation strategy for urban and urbanizing areas should strive to maintain, to the extent possible, regional species diversity. The strategy also must relate to human needs and desires.

Leedy *et al.* (1978) presented guidelines to such planning for (1) site–level design, (2) regional–level design, and (3) design and landscaping in developed areas. Their recommendations for regional–level design are most relevant to the focus of the present report (Fig. 4). At the regional scale, these authors recom-

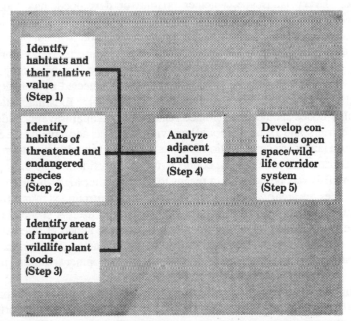

Fig. 4. Flow diagram of basic wildlife planning procedures at the regional level. (From Leedy *et al.* 1978.)

mended focusing on preservation and incorporation of regionally limited and/or unique habitat types in a continuous open space network. They stressed the importance of planners, builders, developers, landscape architects, biologists, and ecologists working together to achieve desirable goals.

Noss (1983) also discussed diversity at different scales, from that observed in a single habitat type to that of a geographic region. He pointed out that a patchwork of different habitat types, and different successional stages, may well maximize local species *richness*, but one should also be concerned with species *composition* at a regional scale. If habitat patches become too small, many area–sensitive species will be lost (see Chapter 3 for a discussion of area–sensitive species). Thus, maximizing only local diversity may operate at the expense of species and communities most in need of protection at the regional level. Argument continues over whether one large preserve or several smaller preserves (of the same total area) is optimal for preservation of regional diversity (see Appendix C for additional references on this topic). For the most part, the focus has been on species number, with little consideration of species composition. Diamond (1976), in discussing human–dominated landscapes, addressed this point in stating, *"The question is not which refuge system contains more total species, but which contains more species that would be doomed to extinction in the absence of refuges."* (emphasis added).

An approach for preserving native diversity that is appropriate at all scales in the landscape was recently proposed by Noss and Harris (1986). These authors pointed out that natural resources are not distributed randomly throughout a landscape. Every landscape, whether pristine or developed, has "nodes" of unusually high conservation value that span the entire range of biological hierarchy as well as particular physical habitats. Examples include a "champion" tree, a red–cockaded woodpecker colony, an undrained swamp, a county park, or a national forest. These nodes should receive top priority for protection, but to function in perpetuity, sites must be buffered, interconnected by corridors, and permitted to interact with surrounding natural habitats. Existing patterns of high–quality nodes should be examined relative to potential travel corridors and dispersal barriers, and a scheme should be devised to utilize and develop the existing pattern into a landscape conservation scheme. The effort should strive to minimize artificial barriers and to maximize connectivity with corridors. The multiple–use module (MUM) was proposed as a means to link together high–quality nodes of diversity. The core area of a MUM is a node of diversity surrounded by multiple–use buffer zones of appropriate type, scale, and intensity of use. A strategy must be developed that emphasizes (a) comprehensive planning aimed at threatened elements or nodes of diversity, (b) integration of nodes into networks of protected and buffer areas, and (c) integration of conservation and development planning for long-term maintenance of environmental quality (Fig. 5).

A quite similar approach, specific to metropolitan areas, has been prepared for Britain (Halcrow Fox & Associates *et al.* 1987). These authors reported that elements of a wildlife conservation program should include: (1) protection of established sites, (2) securing linkages between sites, and (3) ensuring that wildlife

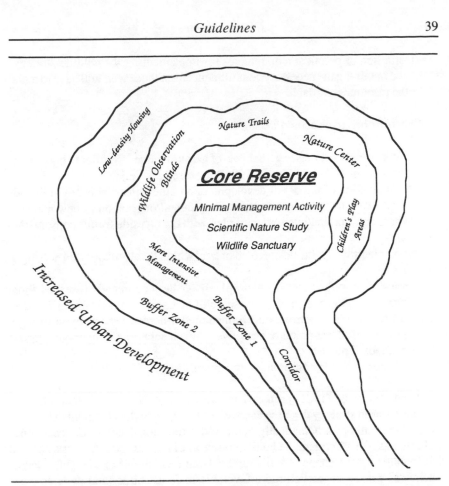

Fig. 5. An urban wildlife reserve, connecting corridor, and buffer zones providing multiple benefits. Adapted from Harris (1984) and Noss (1987b). See also Goldstein *et al.* (1981, 1983); Hoehne (1981); Shaw *et al.* (1986); Hench *et al.* (1987); Schicker (1986, 1987); and Tilghman (1987a).

sites are available to everyone. The basic program framework needs to be established in collaboration with neighboring authorities to ensure a wider context to site evaluation and continuity of wildlife corridors. A "whole city" approach would be most ideal. A general wildlife conservation program to provide the foundation for individual plans for any metropolitan district should include the following:

- An assessment of the wildlife resources of the area. Also the social value (and potential) of those resources.
- Formulation of policies for wildlife conservation. These should be integrated, where appropriate, with other planning objectives.

- Definition of practical requirements for implementing the wildlife strategy, and obtaining the necessary commitments from those who will have to make the resources available.

Specific objectives should include:

- Protection of best sites, e.g., habitats of greatest value. [Similar to high–value "nodes" of Noss and Harris (1986) discussed above.]
- Minimization of impact of development on other sites. This might include modifications to designs to reduce impact and/or creation of new habitat.
- Where appropriate, integration of plan with countryside (rural) conservation areas.
- Maximization of wildlife potential of land within local authority ownership or control.
- Provision for public use. Local people should be encouraged to use the habitat network. However, not every site will be capable of sustaining free and regular access. Control should be instituted, where necessary, by site design, location of access points or attractive footpath networks, or by more rigorous methods if needed.
- Promote wildlife conservation in general.

Goldstein *et al.* (1981) proposed an innovative design scheme that relates to the conservation strategy discussed above. With regard to development in forested areas, these authors schematically compared a traditional layout of rectangular building lots (0.1 ha) for single family houses to triangular lots. Analysis showed that, by altering the shape of building lots from rectangular to triangular, larger patches of woody vegetation more favorable to forest birds (and perhaps other wildlife as well) could be more effectively clumped on private lots. Their design scheme related only to changes in traditional lot configuration and made no assumption of common open space provisions (that is possible in cluster–type development, for example) in the hypothetical development. The basic argument was extended to larger designs in Goldstein *et al.* (1983).

Cluster development offers greater flexibility for maintaining some of the natural land features and habitats than does traditional–type development. Lot sizes, setback requirements, and road rights–of–way are typically reduced, and development is grouped on the most buildable portions of a site with the remainder preserved as open space (Nordstrom 1988, and others). Compared to traditional lot development, clustering generally allows the same overall building density on a site. The two examples below illustrate the greater consideration of wildlife possible with cluster-type development.

The developer of a 17–ha planned development (Hillandale) in Washington, D.C., had a desire to develop his property in an environmentally–sensitive manner. The site was about 75% forested and trees were mostly native hardwoods, including some oaks over 1.2 m in diameter and tulip poplars approximately 4.6 m in girth.

The property was zoned for conventional residential development (rectangular lots), but the developer wished to build clustered units in order to preserve much of the natural terrain and vegetation as open space. With a team of consultants, including wildlife biologists, he proposed, and obtained, a variance from the local authorities to allow a planned unit development (PUD), with clustering, on the site. The plan included habitat corridors linking the open space of Hillandale with two adjacent parks. Franklin and Wilkinson (1986) predicted the impact of the two alternative plans (conventional vs PUD) on breeding birds and other wildlife of the property. Based on their work on site and review of other studies, these investigators concluded that the PUD, if properly managed, would provide better habitat for breeding birds and other wildlife at Hillandale than would conventional development.

On a larger scale, extensive planning was devoted to design of the "new town" of Columbia, Maryland. Development of Columbia is still continuing on 5,670 ha of former forest and farmland about halfway between Baltimore and Washington, D.C. The original new town zoning, approved in May 1965, called for a minimum of 20% open space, a minimum of 15% low density residential properties, and attached housing not to exceed 10%. Over the years, several modifications have been made in zoning, with the overall tendency being to cluster housing more tightly while providing greater amounts of open space. For example, one portion of Columbia, slated for single–family detached housing, included particularly valuable stream valley habitat. Zoning was changed to increase housing density in other parts of Columbia in order to preserve some 405 ha of stream valley habitat as a natural area (Geis 1986).

An issue of considerable importance is how to integrate human preferences and use of urban reserves and corridors with wildlife use. Little research has dealt with balancing these uses. Schicker (1987) reported some interesting results on how children (ages 6–10) relate to wildlife and wildlife habitat of urban–suburban areas. In her study, children were among the most frequent users of neighborhood open space, they played close to home, and among their favorite areas were "wildlands" and vacant lots.

With respect to design criteria, Schicker reported that kids placed high value on outdoor places for play that allowed for personal investigation and manipulation of materials. Large areas were not required, but sites should be centrally located in residential developments buffered by residences instead of by roads, with attention given to both social and physical safety issues. Ideally, a variety of habitats is desirable, including aquatic, forest, field, and edge. According to Schicker, "If one were forced to choose a single neighborhood open space that best suits wildlife and kids simultaneously, it should be a greenbelt park along a stream corridor with small patches or clumps of vegetation and pathways that accommodate bicycle travel. The closer to home, the better."

Schicker also found that, for children in her study, 50% of all outdoor activities directly involved wildlife (e.g., collecting, observing, etc.). And, unlike adults, who typically are most interested in birds and mammals, the children's most favorite

Photo: L.E. Dove

Little research has dealt with balancing human use and enjoyment of urban wildlife reserves and corridors with wildlife use of the areas. See text (Hench *et al.* 1987 and Schicker 1987) for summaries of two studies.

wild animals were the "creepy–crawly" variety such as amphibians, reptiles, and insects. These were mentioned, looked for, and collected more than all others. Such findings have important educational implications in terms of interesting children at an early age in wildlife conservation. Schicker concluded that "Providing places for children to grow up that are both challenging and naturally beautiful can only make them better decision makers about our environmental future." We concur.

Hench *et al.* (1987) addressed the issue of human and wildlife use of regional parks in Montgomery County, Maryland. In 1927, a Maryland state law was passed authorizing the formation of a Maryland–National Capital Park and Planning Commission for the Montgomery County and Prince George's County, Maryland, suburbs of Washington, D.C. The agency coordinates development in the bicounty area, and levies taxes, issues bonds, and condemns property for the purpose of acquiring land for parks, pathways, and other public places.

On 15 December 1968, the Commission approved a resolution requiring at least 66% of each regional park (a park of at least 81 ha) to be maintained in natural areas or conservation areas. The remaining 33% of a regional park may be developed for recreational activities (active–use areas).

Hench *et al.* (1987) proposed the creation of a natural resources management program to better protect and manage natural resources in the parks. According to these authors, natural areas and conservation areas enhance active–use areas by contributing to the character of the latter, by serving as outdoor classrooms for nature study and outdoor laboratories for scientific research, and by providing the tranquil environment that many park users seek. Carefully designed trails––including those for walking, jogging, and horseback riding– –can penetrate the nature–conservation areas. Observation platforms, study blinds, food and cover plots, and feeding stations can facilitate a safe and enjoyable interaction between people and wildlife. In turn, active–use areas can positively impact nature–conservation areas by providing a broad constituency of park users who can be called upon to support the department politically when alternative land–use proposals, originating in other county agencies, threaten a park's integrity.

Hench and his co–workers further recommended that a natural resources concept plan be prepared before preparation of the recreation concept plan during the master planning process for a park. Trade–offs in natural resource and recreation values should be discussed and negotiated. Those recommendations have been formally adopted by the Maryland–National Capital Park and Planning Commission (J.E. Hench, personal communication 1988), and we believe they represent a balance between conserving a park's natural resources while meeting public recreational needs.

Without a doubt, public knowledge, attitudes, and preferences regarding wildlife habitats are important factors contributing to habitat conservation in the metropolitan environment. Little research has been conducted in this area.

Pudelkewicz (1981) studied the visual preference for wildlife habitat and the relationship of particular habitat characteristics to visual preference of residents of Columbia, Maryland. She concluded that good wildlife habitat can be incorporated into residential open space systems in a visually preferred manner and that this can best be accomplished through the support of urban planners and managers, and by landscape architects and wildlife biologists integrating their concepts of good landscape design. In a later study, Adams *et al.* (1984) reported that 94% of the respondents to a Columbia–wide survey felt that wetlands add to the beauty, diversity, and quality of the human living environment and that it would be desirable to design and manage stormwater control basins for fish and wildlife as well as for flood and sediment control if this were feasible from technical and economic standpoints.

During the summer of 1986, Schauman *et al.* (1987) investigated the relationships among knowledge, attitudes, and preferences of Seattle, Washington residents for urban open space with wildlife habitat value. Residents appeared to be able to recognize relative values of habitat for wildlife. However, preference for a natural landscape (i.e., one with greater wildlife value) was inversely related to nearness of such an area to one's home. Residents' knowledge regarding the interaction between wildlife and habitat related somewhat to preference, but this association was weak. The authors suggested that, perhaps through education, this association could be strengthened, resulting in a more informed public with stronger conservation goals for remnant urban habitats.

Photo: M. Saunders

Local public support is an important factor contributing to habitat conservation in the metropolitan environment.

The Tucson, Arizona, metropolitan area serves as a good example where biologists, planners, other professionals, and interested citizens are working together to maintain wildlife and environmental quality values in a rapidly–developing area (Burns *et al.* 1986, Shaw *et al.* 1986, Shaw and Supplee 1987). Three initial steps were undertaken to protect the unique biological communities of Arizona: (1) A statewide habitat evaluation by biologists in 1979, (2) the development of a nongame wildlife branch of the Arizona Game and Fish Department (AGFD) in 1983, and (3) the approval of a policy statement on urban wildlife management by AGFD to promote the development and preservation of urban habitat in 1986.

When the nongame wildlife branch was formed, biologists were given the use of the data management system of The Nature Conservancy that had already located many sensitive and threatened plant and animal species within the state. Today, when AGFD biologists located in urban regions are asked to review development proposals, their evaluation of the project typically includes information from the data base on nongame and threatened or endangered plant and animal species on the site, as well as the more standard impact analysis on local game species.

In 1985, a more comprehensive study of critical and sensitive biological habitats was initiated in the Tucson, Arizona area. Fortuitously, the interests of a number of groups came together to allow the development of a significant urban habitat conservation policy. In particular, the AGFD was able to work with the Pima County Planning and Zoning Department to establish procedures requiring developers and landowners to prepare a site analysis report prior to submission of a rezoning request. Based on a model developed by Boulder County, Colorado,

Tucson developers must submit maps of sensitive wildlife habitats and vegetative communities with their report. To prepare the site analysis report, developers use information obtained from an AGFD biologist on the wildlife values of the site. Following the site analysis report, developers must submit a land use proposal, in which they have the opportunity to "design around" the sensitive areas identified in the site analysis. During the 1985 comprehensive study, the most ecologically–sensitive areas were located on aerial maps of Tucson, and designated by color coded shading on acetate overlays. These sensitive areas were classified as "Class I" or "Class II" Habitats. "Class I Habitat" areas are few in number, are mostly associated with watercourses, and are of primary concern for preservation. They include (1) deciduous riparian woodlands, (2) mesquite bosques, (3) wetlands with adjacent plant cover, (4) important travel corridors for large mammals, and (5) corridors of desert riparian habitat that connect large public reserves surrounding Tucson with the metropolis. (Large national forests and other reserves almost surround Tucson, and provide extensions of undisturbed habitat into developed areas. These important natural corridors protect unique desert songbirds, mammals and plant species, and allow their movement into and out of the Tucson metropolitan area.) The "Class II Habitat" designation was given to sensitive areas somewhat more abundant and not as critical for protection. Thus, regional and local developers have overlay maps and other information available to help them design around the most critical and sensitive ecological habitats of Tucson.

To educate the public about the values of integrating wildlife into the planning process, Shaw *et al.* (1986) developed a descriptive booklet and a regional wildlife habitat map for residents of the Tucson area. The map indicates the Class I and Class II habitats that should be protected, many of which extend into urban neighborhoods. Among the techniques recommended by these investigators for conserving the natural resources of the area are the following:

(1) Protect critical habitat in public ownership by outright purchase of the land. Such areas are usually protected for multiple purposes, particularly riparian areas that are unsuitable for development but are valuable as open space and for recreation and flood control.

(2) Encourage developers to design around sensitive natural features of the site, using ecological principles to reduce the impact of their plans on critical wildlife habitat. These ecological principles include:

    (a) protecting riparian (streamside) vegetation wherever possible,

    (b) protecting continuous corridors of natural vegetation wherever possible, and

    (c) disturbing as little natural vegetation as possible.

To accomplish these goals, developers are advised to develop an open space system early in the planning process to ensure that the most valuable habitats are protected.

(3) Enhance and/or restore wildlife habitat by transplanting or planting additional native plants in the developed landscape. Revegetation techniques are

particularly important in creating corridors by linking open spaces and providing vegetative diversity. Water bodies with nearby vegetative cover are more valuable than ponds without plants, and degraded watercourses can also be converted into amenities for wildlife and people by revegetation.

(4) Create buffer zones of low density housing adjacent to sensitive wildlife areas to minimize human–related disturbances to such areas. Although this simple action is not a substitute for more careful planning that considers the actual biological resources of the area, low density buffer zones do create a gradual transition from protected natural areas to a heavily developed area.

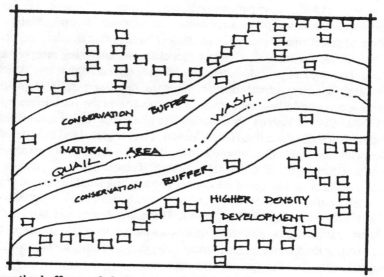

Conservation buffers can help to protect wildlife habitat in a development. (From Shaw *et al.* 1986.)

(5) Use the concept of cluster development as an alternate site design to protect more open space for wildlife. Ideally, open space within developments should be integrated with corridors and reserves of open space beyond the site's boundaries.

(6) Offer incentives to landowners who protect valuable habitats for wildlife. In addition to the tax benefits of conservation easements, a landowner may be allowed to increase the density of housing units in an area of no particular wildlife value, in exchange for not developing in a critical wildlife habitat area.

If a single conservation goal were to be stated by those involved in protecting the natural resources of Tucson, it might be to develop a corridor of interconnected open space for wildlife and people, based upon the riparian habitat available throughout the Tucson area. Significant progress has been made by activities at the local and state level to accomplish this goal. [See Leedy *et al.* (1978, 1981) for further assistance in planning for fish and wildlife in urban and urbanizing areas.]

ADDITIONAL RECOMMENDATIONS

With regard to birds, Robbins (1979) presented 16 recommendations to retain forest–interior species in the breeding bird community. The seven items listed below are most relevant to the objectives of the present report.

- Avoid unnecessary fragmentation of forests.
- Plan cooperatively with adjacent landowners so that maximum repopulation potential of those species that require extensive mature or near mature forest can be achieved.
- In areas where mature forest is limited, consider preserving one or more strategically located mature tracts to serve as sources of avian repopulation.
- Retain vegetational diversity to the extent feasible.
- In smaller tracts (even down to 2 ha or less) it is beneficial to maintain the maximum contiguous woodland with the least amount of edge.
- Management units that approach the shape of a square are more effective in preserving forest–interior birds than are long, narrow ones—especially when managed tracts are small.
- If wooded fragments must be isolated from the forest proper, retain a connecting corridor, such as along a stream; or if a forest tract has already been separated, consider planting a corridor to reconnect it.

Tilghman (1987a), based on research in the northeastern U.S., listed the following recommendations for improving the design and management of urban woodlands for enrichment of the avifauna.

- "Large woodlands (>25 ha) are necessary to maintain a high bird species diversity and thus provide urban dwellers with the opportunity to see a wide variety of birds typical of more rural forests of the region.
- "Maintenance of natural vegetation in the shrub layer can provide an increased number of niches for an increase in number of bird species.
- "Woodlands with a variety of microhabitats, such as small scattered openings and some form of water in or adjacent to the woods, can provide nesting and feeding sites for a variety of birds. Patches of pines or hemlocks and wetland areas within the woods can also increase the number of birds in the area.
- "Wherever possible, buildings immediately adjacent to the woodlands (within 90 m) should be kept to a minimum.
- "Trail systems should be limited in scope. Instead of a fine network of trails throughout the woods, a few well–marked trails providing human access to particular portions of the woods should be maintained."

DeGraaf (1987), drawing from his own research on birds and that of others, presented guidelines designed particularly for use by landscape architects. He pointed out that, with consideration to the habitat requirements of birds, species richness can be enhanced. He recommended that the following factors be considered by landscape architects, planners, and others interested in enhancing bird life in the urban environment.

- Retain, insofar as possible, some of the predevelopment fields and woodlots. Retention of woodlots will provide habitat for some forest birds, especially cavity nesters if trees containing decayed wood are not removed or pruned. Planted trees, no matter how mature or abundant, apparently do not replace natural forest stands as habitat for insectivorous birds.
- Maximize patch size of woody vegetation. In the planted environment, maximizing the crown volumes of trees and shrubs is likely the one management practice or goal that will yield the greatest increases in breeding bird species richness.
- Plant trees, shrubs, and other vegetation of known food or cover value to birds.

Planning and design guidelines for optimizing the value of man–made urban stormwater control ponds as wetland reserves for wildlife were summarized by Adams and Dove (1984) and Adams *et al.* (1986) and are presented below. (See also Milligan 1985.)

- Where possible, impoundments for stormwater control should aim to retain water rather than merely detain it.
- Pond design must meet applicable stormwater control criteria, including legal requirements.
- Natural resources personnel, including biologists, should be consulted during the planning and design stages.
- All potential pond locations should be evaluated to select the most suitable site in relation to the developed area and surroundings, and in recognition of physical, social, economic, and biologic factors.
- There should be an adequate drainage area to provide a dependable source of water for the intended year–round use of the pond, considering seepage and evaporation losses.
- The soil on site must have sufficient bearing strength to support the dam without excessive consolidation and be impermeable enough to hold water.
- The pond site should be located in an area where disturbances to valuable existing wildlife habitat by construction activities will be avoided or minimized.
- Impoundments with gently sloping sides (on the order of 10:1) are preferable to impoundments with steep slopes. Gently sloping sides will encourage the establishment of marsh vegetation. Vegetation will provide food and cover for wildlife and help to enhance water quality. Impoundments with gently sloping sides also are safer than steep–sided ponds for children who might enter the impoundments, and gently sloping sides facilitate use by terrestrial wildlife.
- Water depth should not exceed 61 cm for 25–50% of the water surface area, with approximately 50–75% having a depth not less than 1.1–1.2 m. A greater

Photo: L.W. Adams

If properly designed and managed, man–made urban stormwater control ponds can provide wetland reserves for wildlife. See text for details.

depth may be advisable for more northern areas subject to greater ice thickness.

- An emergent vegetation/open water ratio of about 50:50 should be maintained (Hobaugh and Teer 1981, Weller 1978).
- For larger impoundments (≥ 2 ha), the construction of one or more small islands is recommended. The shape and position of islands should be designed to help direct water flow within the impoundment. Water flow around and between islands can help to oxygenate the water and prevent stagnation. Water quality can be enhanced by a flow–through system where water is continually flushed through the impoundment (Harris *et al.* 1981). Islands should be gently sloped, and the tops should be graded to provide good drainage. Appropriate vegetative cover should be established to prevent erosion and provide bird nesting cover. Consideration should be given to including an overland flow area in the design of large impoundments. In a California study (Duffield 1986), the overland flow subsystem (pond–overland flow–pond subsystem) with shallow water and mudflat areas attracted the greatest diversity of waterbirds.
- Impoundments should be designed with the capability to regulate water levels, including complete drainage, and with facilities for cleaning, if necessary.
- Locating permanent–water impoundments near existing wetlands generally will enhance the wildlife values of impoundments.

5

APPROACHES TO PROVIDING WILDLIFE RESERVES AND CORRIDORS IN THE METROPOLITAN ENVIRONMENT

In Chapters 3 and 4, we reviewed the current state of knowledge regarding habitat reserves and corridors and presented some guidelines to ecological landscape planning and wildlife conservation. Our goal here is to present some specific examples of how various approaches to establishing reserves and corridors have been implemented successfully.

A number of methods are available for individuals and private and public organizations to acquire and protect natural areas that may be valuable as corridors and reserves in the urban/suburban environment. In many instances, there are tax incentives to encourage the landowner to set aside tracts of land for conservation purposes, particularly when the land that is preserved is recognized as having value for the public. Among the approaches that have been used to establish corridors and reserves in metropolitan areas are the following: Land may be (1) purchased outright; (2) obtained as a donation by the owner; (3) traded for more ecologically–desirable land; (4) protected through a voluntary registration agreement with the owner; (5) protected with a legally–binding management agreement with the owner; (6) secured as a conservation easement; (7) protected by law for its ecological importance, such as critical habitat for threatened and endangered species, or wetlands areas; (8) protected by law for its historical or aesthetic significance; (9) obtained as mitigation for development elsewhere; (10) set aside as open space as a requirement of development; (11) regulated by zoning requirements; and (12) obtained by other means (e.g., purchased with monies from a real estate transfer tax).

Following are examples that show how the various methods have been used to set aside land for urban reserves. Many of the examples illustrate the work of The Nature Conservancy (TNC), a private nonprofit, scientific and educational organization, dedicated to identifying, protecting, and maintaining examples of unique ecosystems. The Conservancy owns and manages some 1,000 preserves in this hemisphere, and it has transferred management of additional protected areas to other public and private groups. In acquiring preserve lands, TNC utilizes most of the methods just mentioned, sometimes in ingenious combinations. Urban land conservation is also an expanding activity of governmental agencies, because of the need to provide open–space land for urban–suburban residents, and to protect natural resources within developing areas. Some of the examples describe the work of public agencies to include conservation areas within their land–use plans.

OUTRIGHT PURCHASE

Ring Mountain, California

The California state branch of The Nature Conservancy was able to obtain the majority of the land in an urban preserve at Ring Mountain by the outright purchase of several land parcels. The Conservancy describes Ring Mountain as "a biological island atop the Tiburon Peninsula," noting that it is the only urban preserve among the Conservancy's 36 protected areas in California. Located in Marin County, 24.1 km north of downtown San Francisco, Ring Mountain rises 183 m on the west side of the Tiburon Peninsula. Along with magnificent views of the skyline of San Francisco and other scenery of the Bay Area, the Mountain is home to seven indigenous rare or endangered plant species. The area also has unusual geological features and a diversity of wildlife; and at least one plant species and one species of blind harvestman spider that exist nowhere else on earth. Of historical and educational interest are Indian petroglyphs (rock drawings) and other evidence of early human activity on the site. Botanists, geologists, archaeologists, and school and university groups have long visited Ring Mountain for research and study. In response to the threat of development on the Mountain, the Conservancy obtained ownership and management rights to a 122.3–ha property by giving the owners a low–interest loan worth $240,000. The owners gave the Conservancy complete title to 17 ha and management rights to an additional 105.3 ha for a 5–year period. A 30.4 ha tract was purchased from another owner, forming a contiguous preserve of 152.7 ha on Ring Mountain.

Mud Pond: Purchase *and* Mitigation

An acquisition of land in the fast–growing town of Williston, Vermont, demonstrates how complex an outright–purchase transaction may become. It is also an excellent example of public and private groups working together to form a nature reserve, because cooperation among a total of seven organizations was required to accomplish the arrangement. The town of Williston worked in concert with The Nature Conservancy to acquire a 119.5–ha tract that included Mud Pond, a significant 14.2–ha wetland area, and habitat of the threatened four–toed salamander. Because of mitigation requirements placed upon him, a developer in the town was persuaded to contribute about $63,000 toward the purchase price of $275,000 raised by the Conservancy. In exchange, the Conservancy agreed to meet the developer's mitigation requirements by preserving agricultural land on the Mud Pond property. Williston faces intense development pressures and the preserve will form the core of a Conservation District that can be enlarged in coming years. The town will manage the area, and will raise monies to repurchase the land from the Conservancy within 5 years for $137,000, by charging recreation fees or by bonding (The Nature Conservancy, Vermont Field Office 1987).

Maximizing Monies for Purchase

By transferring management responsibilities to other groups, TNC keeps its costs low and uses available monies for the outright purchase of important sites that cannot be obtained any other way. Thus, the Connecticut Chapter of the Conservancy manages about 40 different tracts of land, and has turned over 70 other tracts to about 90 local land trusts for protection. Occasionally, a local trust will fail to carry out its stewardship, and the preserves revert back to the Conservancy. To date, more than 400,000 ha of TNC–owned land have been transferred to public agencies for management. The federal government has accepted about 324,000 ha, and the remainder has gone to various states (Gilbert 1986).

Other Programs

The Missouri Department of Conservation has a successful Urban Biology Program, which was created in 1978. Among other things, significant natural habitats have been acquired in both the Kansas City and St. Louis metropolitan areas. Typically, acquired tracts are leased to a local parks department for management. Leases include provisions to protect the natural qualities of the tracts and encourage only passive types of recreational uses. In addition, management plans, including recommended practices, are developed (Werner and Tylka 1984).

TAX INCENTIVES

Donations of Property

To encourage individuals to donate gifts to conservation and other charitable causes, the federal tax laws allow benefits in the form of tax shelters on the donor's income tax, capital gains tax, and/or estate tax. The gifts must be made to a nonprofit organization as defined by section 501 (c) (3) of the tax code, or to a government agency, and may be made during or after the donor's lifetime. A nonprofit organization may also serve as an intermediary to a government agency when a donation is made, and as a land steward in other arrangements (Montana Land Reliance 1979).

The Connecticut Chapter of The Nature Conservancy (personal communication 1988) stated that TNC owns 3,240 ha of preserves, and protects (but does not own) an additional 3,240 ha of natural sites in that state. The majority of the land in Connecticut preserves was obtained as donations from the owners, and most of the acreage is in, or close to, developed areas.

The National Audubon Society operates a notable sanctuary program. Many of the 80 or so Audubon sanctuaries—not including those owned and independently operated by Audubon chapters— –are in or near urban areas (Leedy and Adams 1987). Most of these were donated to Audubon by persons interested in preserving habitat for birds and other wildlife. Some examples of sanctuaries in or near developed areas include: Dauphin Island, Alabama; Schlitz Audubon Center, Wisconsin; Audubon Center and Fairchild Wildflower Garden, Connecticut; and Starr Ranch, California.

Trade Agreements

The Nature Conservancy has a "Trade Lands Program," by which tax–deductible gifts of property that have low ecological value may be sold at fair–market value in order to purchase more desirable natural areas. The donor of tradeland property may direct how the proceeds are to be spent. Occasionally, corporations donate urban land in industrial or residential areas to conservation organizations, such as the Conservancy, and this valuable real estate can be marketed accordingly. TNC has received trade lands with a value of about $35 million, while businesses received corporate tax benefits for donating such properties as obsolete factory sites and land left over from development projects (Gilbert 1986).

Private landowners have also contributed to the Trade Lands Program, and in addition to land, homes and their contents may be donated and resold under this program. Recently, in Talbot County, Maryland, an historic waterfront estate, including a home that contained many valuable antiques, was willed to the Conservancy. In accordance with the donor's wishes, the home and the antiques will be sold at auction, and the profit will be used to purchase nature preserves in the State of Maryland. Forested acreage within the estate will be preserved by the Conservancy to protect the endangered Delmarva fox squirrel present on the site (The Nature Conservancy, Maryland–Delaware Office 1988).

Conservation Easements

A fundamental principle of land ownership conceives of real property not as tangible land and buildings, but as a group of abstract "rights." The landowner owns what can be seen as well as what cannot be seen. What cannot be seen includes "air rights," "mineral rights," "access rights," and the "right to possess or develop any of these" (Barrett and Livermore 1983). The owner can hold these rights or he can transfer any or all of them to others.

Easements also have a long history in legal theory. An easement conveys a limited interest in real property from the property owner to another–who becomes the "easement owner" or the "grantee." When easements are adapted to conservation purposes, the landowner gives up the right to develop the land, while retaining his other rights in the property. The grantee of the easement becomes responsible for enforcing the terms of the easement, and often, leaves the land in its natural state. In effect, by setting up a conservation easement, development rights are transferred so that those rights will *not* be exercised.

When development rights are donated (often to a private, nonprofit conservation organization, but it may be to a public agency), the landowner may claim some

Habitat of the endangered Delmarva fox squirrel is being protected in Maryland under the Trade Lands Program of The Nature Conservancy.

value of the conservation easement for a tax deduction. Both open space and historical buildings can be protected with this type of easement, but the Internal Revenue Service (IRS) will look for assurance that a conservation contribution will result in a substantial benefit to the public. According to Barrett (1983), the gift must meet the tests of one of the four "conservation purpose requirements" to qualify for a federal tax deduction. These four requirements are: (1) Recreation or education, (2) historic preservation, (3) protection of significant habitats or ecosystems, and (4) open space lands. [Under category (4), the IRS recognizes the scenic value of land, and considers urban as well as rural landscapes worthy of exemption for their scenic beauty.]

The Nature Conservancy has incorporated the conservation easement as one of the techniques used in its work to protect natural areas. On Botany Bay Island, South Carolina, a resort development was kept to a maximum of eight homes on 16.2 ha in exchange for a conservation easement on 179.4 ha of ecologically–significant beaches and dunes. The original schedule had called for the development of 300 residential units on this barrier island that provides nesting habitat for the threatened loggerhead sea turtle. Valued at $2.55 million, the Conservancy purchased Botany Bay Island for $1 million and, almost simultaneously, resold the property for $1.2 million–subject to a conservation easement–to a private corporation. Thus, protection of the island was ensured at no cost to TNC, and resale profits will be used to fund a program to monitor the nesting sea turtles. The easement will also protect two uncommon plant species that were identified on the island. A similar easement was obtained by TNC to protect a natural area of Hilton Head, an island also undergoing development along South Carolina's coast.

The Maryland Environmental Trust holds a scenic easement on this 6.5–ha, mostly wooded, residential property in Potomac, Maryland.

According to Roger Jones of the South Carolina Nature Conservancy's Field Office (personal communication 1988), conservation–easement donations work well when property values are high but the land is not well–suited to development, such as in wetland areas. The landowner can ensure the protection of the site while obtaining a significant tax benefit for himself. The Conservancy usually acquires property, continues a fee simple ownership, and transfers it to a public agency or private organization for management. Because of the high cost of buying and maintaining Botany Bay Island, the Conservancy chose to resell the preserve with the development restrictions of a conservation easement in perpetuity (State of South Carolina 1987; South Carolina Nature Conservancy 1987).

The nonprofit Natural Area Preservation Association (NAPA), Dallas, Texas, also has received conservation easements from private donors, and some tracts are located in urban areas. For example, in 1986, a private landowner donated an easement to 6.5 wooded hectares in Nacogdoches, Texas, to the Association. The area is now known as the Banita Creek Reserve, a valuable urban wildlife refuge. The Association will receive full title to the property on the owner's death. An easement also is held by NAPA on the 16.2–ha James K. Allen Nature Sanctuary, in Fort Worth, Texas.

The federal government has used conservation easements to protect crucial wildlife habitat without the expense of outright purchase, such as "pothole" waterfowl breeding areas in the Midwest. It has also provided funds to state and local governments to acquire scenic and open space easements as, for instance, along highways. The California State Department of Parks and Recreation has used the conservation–easement technique since 1933 to restrict the use of lands in and adjacent to state parks, although federal funds have seldom had to be used because most California parklands have been donated (Barrett and Livermore 1983). In California and some other states, conservation easements must be granted for not less than 10 years, and ideally these easements are granted in perpetuity. (See Diehl and Barrett 1988 for further discussion of conservation easements.)

The Case of Tax–Exempt Cemetery Lands

Behrens (1972) discussed tax exemptions as they apply to cemeteries and associated cemetery lands. Although individual states differ in exemption laws, cemetery property generally is exempt from taxation because burial is considered an activity necessary for the public welfare. Roadways, trails, garden areas, and other real property associated with cemetery operations are also considered exempt if no profit comes to the cemetery owner from these operations. These tax laws become crucial when considering the potential importance of cemetery habitat to urban wildlife.

The value of urban cemeteries as wildlife refuges has long been recognized. Cemeteries represent a form of land use that is nearly permanent for, once established, they are seldom relocated. This permanency increases the value of cemetery lands as wildlife habitat, because trees and shrubs and other natural features that are landscaping elements of most cemeteries can be allowed to mature. They provide food, cover, and living space for wildlife, and in older cemeteries, large trees may attract arboreal birds, and cavity–nesting birds and mammals. In Mount Auburn Cemetery in Cambridge, Massachusetts, the early proprietors deliberately planted trees that were attractive to birds, and although its primary purpose was as a cemetery, Mount Auburn became noteworthy for its flora and fauna. Now more than 150 years old, this urban cemetery has been used by bird watchers for years and, according to Howard (1987), more than 200 different bird species have been recorded on the grounds. Amphibians and reptiles, relatively rare in urban areas, may also survive in appropriate cemetery habitat, where the lack of human disturbance may provide the isolation needed for some species. Cemeteries are especially important urban refuges when they are close to other natural areas and are a link in the wildlife corridor system of a city.

Cemeteries may be useful as refuges for plant and animal species that are threatened or endangered elsewhere. Such species may already be present on cemetery land, or may be introduced there for protection. One group of German investigators (Sukopp *et al.* 1979) has called for preserving naturalized vegetation that springs up in urban areas, because it may be better adapted to surviving in cities. Sukopp and his colleagues suggested that "field laboratories" to study and to

Photo: L.E. Dove

Thoughtful landscaping of cemeteries can enhance wildlife habitat in the metropolitan environment.

preserve new forms of plants and even new ecosystems could be located in protected urban sites such as the less–frequented areas of old cemeteries. Many cemeteries have areas set aside for expansion that are not visited by the public, which would be particularly valuable for protecting rare flora *and* fauna.

Behrens (1972) pointed out that cemetery areas held for future use are not necessarily considered tax–exempt by the various states. However, in some states, such as Minnesota, certain embellishment of these areas, such as the growing of flowers, weighs in favor of exemption if other requirements are met. Cemetery managers anxious to preserve the tax–exempt status of these passively–held lands might be persuaded to embellish them with plants that are wildlife–attractive. An obvious choice would be to grow flowering plants specific to rare insects such as some of the butterflies.

The California Code allows cemetery property to be "planted, landscaped, arborized or maintained, *if such planting, landscaping, arborizing or maintenance is incident to the burial purpose*, does *not* produce gross receipts for the claimant and is for the purpose of embellishing adjacent cemetery property, preserving the appearance of the property and the surrounding area, *preventing soil erosion*, or similar purposes" (*in* Behrens 1972). With a few changes in planning and vegetation management, cemetery operators in California and elsewhere would be in compliance with the law while encouraging more wildlife during the "planting, landscaping, arborizing, or maintaining" of cemeteries. As trees and shrubs needed to be replaced, new ones with wildlife value could be selected. Ground covers could be used that required less mowing. Plants could be chosen that slow soil erosion while also providing wildlife food and cover.

Tax–code enforcers expect that cemetery land held passively will eventually be used exclusively for burial purposes. However, urban planners and cemetery administrators have recently recognized the potential for auxiliary uses of cemetery lands for urban residents, who have limited access to open space, but could have the opportunity to experience a natural setting in urban cemeteries. Although the concept is still somewhat controversial (American Cemetery Association, personal communication 1988), some cemeteries have allowed recreational pursuits such as active sports, fishing, and art exhibits within their grounds. As long as the primary purpose of the land for burial is maintained, the creative use of both the developed and undeveloped portions of cemeteries seems to fit in with the established tax codes. From a conservation standpoint, the public demand for more open space and the multiple–use of cemeteries for this purpose is encouraging. The addition of heterogeneous plantings will make the cemetery landscape more interesting for people and provide more habitat for wildlife. It may be necessary to restrict recreational opportunities only in those cemeteries with remnant populations of plants and animals.

PROTECTION OF ECOLOGICALLY–SIGNIFICANT AREAS BY LAW

Connecticut Wetland Regulations

The State of Connecticut and local Connecticut municipalities have strong wetland protection regulations. Currently, all but 13 of Connecticut's 169 towns regulate freshwater wetlands at the local level (Aurelia 1987). Because of strong wetland protection regulations, development pressure has been directed to upland areas. A conservation zone subdivision often results, as was the case for the 1976 Old Stone Bridge subdivision. This development, on 34 ha in a 0.8–ha residential zone, could have resulted in 35 0.8–ha residential lots with only 15% (5.3 ha) set aside as open space. However, the developer chose to submit a conservation zone proposal that ultimately resulted in 41 0.4–ha lots and 14.6 ha of open space. Two critical stream corridors and associated wetlands and ponds were preserved within the 14.6 ha of conservation land, now permanently protected by a local land trust. In 1986, 10 years after development, all wetland–watercourse corridors within the 14.6 ha of open space remained relatively undisturbed.

State of Maryland, Chesapeake Bay Critical Areas Commission

The Maryland Critical Areas Program resulted from a 1984 state law requiring the development of management programs to protect the quality of fish, wildlife, and plant habitats of the Chesapeake Bay area. State legislators recognized that development and other human activity within the watershed of the Bay were having a detrimental impact on water quality, as well as threatening forests, wetlands, and other plant and wildlife habitats. The uplands within 405 m of tidal waters were designated as "critical areas," and, with criteria developed by a 25–member Chesapeake Bay Critical Area Commission, counties and municipalities with tidal areas were required to set up programs to protect those critical areas. The Commission also helps to monitor the implementation of the various county and municipal programs. Among the criteria developed by the Commission were specific requirements to protect wildlife corridors and forested areas utilized by forest–interior–dwelling breeding birds. Also, shoreline urban areas were "encouraged to establish, with the assistance from the State, programs for...enhancement of biological resources...for their positive effects on water quality and urban wildlife habitat." Planners who must work within the programs are able to call upon state biologists and other professionals, and existing natural resource information, to help make decisions at the local level.

Performance Zoning

Performance Zoning is used by planners to control development by setting up Performance Standards instead of the more conventional use–categories of separate districts. One type of Performance Zoning is the *bufferyard*, helpful in separating adjacent land areas whose purposes are incompatible. Bufferyards are plantings that separate, for example, commercial from residential districts, and bufferyard criteria may specify the width of the buffer and the type of plant materials to be used. Bufferyards often function to mitigate conflicts involving access, noise, light and glare, and air pollution. The zoning ordinance to develop bufferyards may be comprehensive enough to increase the amount of open space in an urban/suburban community, and, where the vegetation is planted linearly, could provide a continuous corridor system within a developed area.

In Lake County, Illinois, a community may set aside 3 to 8% of the developing land in bufferyards, which could significantly enhance the amount of wildlife habitat. The model performance zoning ordinance in Lake County provides a classification table that allows the planner to determine the bufferyard requirement, and the developer is then given a number of options to fulfill the requirement. The number of plants required varies inversely with the width of the buffer—e.g., a 12.1–m buffer for a 121.5–m lot would require five canopy trees, 10 smaller understory trees, and 16 shrubs. A 8.1–m buffer would require 19 canopy trees, 18 understory trees, and 27 shrubs. (A structure such as a fence can sometimes be used to reduce the width of the buffer.)

Traditionally, bufferyards were treated as an extension of nearby lawns, and it was expected that hedges and grass would be kept trimmed. However, the American Planning Association (APA) has promoted the idea that bufferyards, particularly those that will form dense woodlands, should be designed and maintained as natural landscapes. They also recommended choosing ground covers that require minimal maintenance. If followed, both of these suggestions would substantially increase habitat for wildlife in bufferyards. Finally, because the benefits of natural landscaping may not be initially obvious to some homeowners, the APA recommended that property owners in the development be informed of the types of plants used in bufferyards. This precaution may avoid conflicts later concerning bufferyard maintenance (American Planning Association 1980).

The Real–Estate Transfer Tax

Maryland Program Open Space

An innovative approach to providing public open spaces, natural resource lands, and recreational areas in Maryland (called Program Open Space) was initiated in 1969. The concept was simple and practical—to tax property sales contributing to the decline of natural lands and use the funds obtained for land acquisition and development of outdoor recreation areas. Thus, in a state with an expanding human population, increased land development (reflected through real estate property sales) would result in more protected open space. By law of 1 July 1969, a transfer tax of 0.5% of a property's purchase price was imposed on most real estate transactions including personal, commercial, and industrial property sales. The original legislation provided for the purchase of land only, with the exception that Baltimore City could use its share for development of recreational facilities.

Photo: M. Saunders

Maryland's Program Open Space is an innovative approach to providing public open spaces in an urbanizing environment. See text for details.

However, in 1971, the law was amended to permit local governments to use some open space monies (50% of the local share) for the development of outdoor recreation areas. The state's portion of the fund has been used to purchase state parks and forests, wildlife management areas, natural environmental areas, natural resource management areas, and fish management areas. Through 1986, nearly $180 million had been allocated to state land acquisition and, as of 1 July 1985, some 128,600 ha of state lands had been purchased (about 42% of this total being state forests, 26% wildlife management areas, 26% state parks, and the remainder spread among the other categories listed above). Some $190 million had been provided to local governments under Program Open Space. Examples of local projects include nature centers, trails, hunting areas, picnic areas, playgrounds, and camping areas, among others. In 1987, $24 million were directed to the program. By law, one–half of this total was designated for state land acquisition, agricultural land preservation easements, and a direct grant to Baltimore City for park acquisition, development, or maintenance. The remaining $12 million were distributed to local subdivisions for park acquisitions and development. The Report of the President's Commission on Americans Outdoors recognized Program Open Space as a "national model" to accomplish natural land preservation in a state that is experiencing rapid growth (Maryland Department of Natural Resources 1986).

Nantucket Land Bank

Nantucket Island, off Massachusetts' coast, enacted a 2% real estate transfer tax in 1983 that has generated generous funding to purchase and protect open space on the small resort island. Local planning officials and conservation groups consider the tax crucial to preserving open space. Within 3 years of state legislation enacting the tax, the Nantucket Land Bank Commission had collected more than $6 million from 3,005 real estate transfers. In 1985, the commission issued $11.5 million in tax-free bonds, with $4.5 million backed by the town, to purchase open space. By 1986, 289.2 ha of land, totaling 2.5% of the island, had been acquired. The acquisitions included several ponds, about 36 ha of moors, 4 ha of ocean beach, a 64–ha golf course, and a town park. The goal of the land bank is to preserve 15% of Nantucket Island. At least five northeastern states are looking into legislation needed to allow local governments to implement a special transfer tax for similar purposes. (American Planning Association 1985, Klein 1986.)

Transferable Development Rights (TDRs)

Los Angeles Redevelopment Plan

In order to achieve the redevelopment plan for downtown Los Angeles, the city instituted a plan whereby excess development rights may be sold and transferred from land or buildings in an area where the city wants to limit or prevent development, to other property owners. The Transferable Development Rights (TDR) program allows development rights to be separated from open space and historic buildings (as in a conservation easement), and the rights sold for use in an area scheduled for high–density development. Among the TDRs completed was one used to acquire land for a new park in downtown Los Angeles (American Planning Association 1984).

Maryland TDRs

Local governments in the State of Maryland have similar authority to transfer by sale the right to develop land. TDRs have encouraged historic preservation in many urban areas, and are intended also to protect areas with important natural resources from development, as well as to preserve agricultural land (American Planning Association 1986).

Other Examples of Ecosystem Protection by Law

By protecting or regulating the use of open space with potential wildlife value, land development ordinances can affect wildlife favorably. Medford Township, New Jersey, undertook a thorough environmental planning study and developed an ordinance package that required developers to demonstrate that new projects would not cause ecological damage to the area.

Fish and wildlife habitats are protected from dredging and filling operations or from substance pollution through the permitting process, a regulatory control system administered by the Army Corps of Engineers and the U.S. Environmental Protection Agency.

Some states require environmental impact statements prior to development, which can also help protect wildlife habitat. Although not a true regulatory control, EISs may ensure protection of wildlife in individual projects (Leedy *et al.* 1978).

VOLUNTARY REGISTRATIONS

NIUW Urban Wildlife Sanctuary Program

The Urban Wildlife Sanctuary Program of the National Institute for Urban Wildlife (NIUW) is an example of a voluntary registration program that can increase the amount of reserves and corridors in developed areas. Initiated in 1987, the program is designed to establish and certify a network of urban wildlife sanctuaries on public and privately–owned lands to (1) enhance urban wildlife habitat, (2) promote an appreciation and understanding of urban wildlife and its

The City of Fort Collins, Colorado, is certified as an urban wildlife sanctuary by the National Institute for Urban Wildlife. Formal recognition of the value of wildlife and its habitat within the city is contained in Resolution 87–92, adopted by the City Council on 7 July 1987. The city's Division of Natural Resources is responsible for identifying and monitoring the protection of wildlife habitat within the municipality.

habitat needs, and (3) recognize private and public landowners who dedicate their properties to wildlife. The program is broad and applies to properties of individuals, neighborhood associations, community organizations, cities and towns, corporations, and developers (National Institute for Urban Wildlife, undated).

TNC Voluntary Registration of Sites

There are a number of examples of the voluntary registration of sites by landowners with The Nature Conservancy. A voluntary registration begins when TNC notifies a landowner that his land contains a feature that should be protected. In Connecticut, a federally–protected bird, the piping plover, was found nesting on 10 sites on public beaches. The towns owning the beaches agreed to voluntarily register and protect the sites with the help of the Conservancy. A public education program is an important component of the process, with volunteers working on the beaches in summertime to inform visitors about the need to protect the nest sites. In one instance, a warden has been hired to patrol a sensitive area. Another TNC voluntary registration agreement exists with the Bradley International Airport near Hartford, where interesting grassland birds on the site are protected (The Nature Conservancy, Connecticut Chapter, personal communication 1988).

Other Voluntary Registry Programs

The Nature Conservancy and the Connecticut Department of Environmental Protection operate a joint program, the Natural Heritage Registry, to encourage the preservation of significant natural areas held by private landowners. To be eligible for the Registry, one or more of the following natural features must be present on the site: (1) Habitat for species of plants and animals that are rare in Connecticut; (2) typical examples of native plant vegetation of Connecticut; (3) outstanding natural features such as traprock ridges or bogs. A data base will aid in tracking the program as it gets further underway.

The National Wildlife Federation operates a Backyard Wildlife Habitat Program. That program's goal is ". . .to educate and motivate the public to develop and maintain suitable habitat for a diversity of native animal and plant species" (Tufts 1987). A number of state wildlife agencies with urban programs have initiated similar programs, e.g., Kansas (Schaefer 1987) and Washington (Penland 1987).

OTHER PROGRAMS TO INCREASE URBAN RESERVES

The Work of Public Agencies

In Boulder County, Colorado

State and local governments have the opportunity to significantly influence the design of urban corridors and reserves, and ultimately, the conservation of urban wildlife. These public agencies have a geographical overview of land management activities within their realm, and work on a large enough scale to protect land areas that will provide the habitat needs of many wildlife species. Local zoning regulations also are available to give them the "clout" to determine how planners and developers will use the land. During their review of designs for development projects, governmental agencies can pay attention to how wildlife needs fit into the plans, along with the traditional concerns of providing humans with water, sewage disposal, and transportation (Hallock 1986).

The local government of Boulder County, Colorado, has taken deliberate steps to coordinate land management activities with wildlife needs. The county's experience indicates that an important initial step in the process is to survey the areawide flora and fauna, and to map the distribution of their habitats. Federal regulations protect threatened or endangered species, but potential impacts of development on other local plant and wildlife populations of interest should also be considered. If "critical habitats" are identified and mapped early, developers and planners can often work around these locations before their projects undergo review.

Boulder County is situated north of Denver at a variety of elevations within the Rocky Mountain range, and encompasses eight incorporated cities. In 1978, following a period of rapid population growth, the county adopted a comprehensive plan to stop the decline in numbers of many wildlife species. In fact, Boulder County set a goal of saving every resident and breeding wildlife species "of local concern" then existing within county lands. This was to be accomplished by having local areas protect representative samples of each native habitat which, presumably, would protect examples of most wildlife species. Criteria were drawn up to define "critical wildlife habitat," and a local wildlife data base and habitat map were assembled from field data collected by the Colorado Division of Wildlife, University of Colorado, county staff, local wildlife organizations, and from historical records. Because of its unique geography, the county includes wildlife habitats as diverse as grassland, riparian, open woodland, forest, and alpine tundra. A total of 3,645 ha of critical habitat was assigned to the comprehensive plan, and an additional 28,350 ha were mapped as "environmental conservation areas" because they supported populations of large mammals such as elk for winter range and migration routes. Together, these critical areas encompassed 17% of the total land area of Boulder County. As more data are collected on the status and distribution of local species, the comprehensive planning maps are adjusted accordingly as a guide for potential developers. Because the county has placed the responsibility for protecting wildlife at the local level, county planners are directly involved and they use a variety of zoning regulations, subdivision provisions, and open space purchase plans to protect critical wildlife habitats. These might include the use of conservation easements, density transfers, public purchase, and cooperative management agreements. Although there is no county law that forbids activity in critical areas, the planning staff has a goal of keeping development away from critical habitats insofar as possible. An example of the use of the comprehensive plan occurred when a 54–unit development was planned on 364.5 ha of land that included one of only four known great blue heron rookeries in Colorado. Prior to development, sand and gravel activities were also being carried out in a floodplain on the property. After input from wildlife biologists, a compromise development plan was worked out that prohibited sand and gravel operations when the herons were in residence, and no extractions were ever to be made within 91.5 m of the rookery. The plan also prohibited residential development and the presence of roads or trails within 305 m of the rookery. The site of the rookery will be jointly managed by the homeowners' association of the subdivision, and the Colorado Natural Areas Program (Hallock 1986).

In Portland, Oregon

Planning activities in the State of Oregon are conducted within the framework of 19 "Planning Goals" set up by a statewide land use body. In 1973, the Land Conservation and Development Commission established Goal 15, the Willamette River Greenway, to "... protect, conserve, enhance and maintain the natural, scenic, historical, agricultural, economic and recreational qualities of lands" along the Willamette, a major river that traverses several cities of Oregon (Houck 1987).

Inventories were conducted of fish and wildlife habitats and other significant ecological or scenic resources along the river. These data are available to the planners and government officials who review land use applications and designate appropriate activities along the river and Greenway. In Portland, several areas of significant wildlife habitat were identified during the inventory, including the Oaks Bottom area, now a wildlife refuge, with a variety of habitats, and a diversity of flora and fauna. These areas were subsequently acquired for protection and, because they are close together, provide a corridor for the movement of wildlife along the river.

Plans call for two recreational trail systems to provide access for hikers and bikers near most of the interesting natural areas along the lower Willamette. Property owners are responsible for constructing the trail on their land, and landscaping standards include an emphasis on native plants with some wildlife value. Public participation and education programs help ensure a continuing interest in the protection and enhancement of the Willamette River Greenway. (Houck 1986, 1987).

In Albuquerque, New Mexico

The City Council of Albuquerque, New Mexico, has adopted a complex plan to acquire a 3,402–ha conservation area that includes a state park, pristine canyons and arroyos, and archaeological treasures. Within the proposed conservation area and within city limits is a 27.4–km–long cliff face, or escarpment, that contains more than 15,000 Indian petroglyphs, and dozens of archaeological and historical sites. The plan would preserve the unique natural and historical features of the area, and provide recreational opportunities for the urban public. A "design overlay zone" sets forth criteria for development at the edge of the escarpment, and for roads, streets, and drainage facilities. A "development impact area" extends 107 m from

The City of Toledo, Iowa, has formulated plans to enhance wildlife habitat in its 16.2–ha Toledo Heights Park. More natural areas are planned, including reestablishment of a 1.6–ha prairie.

the base of the escarpment face and includes everything with a slope of 9% or greater. A "protected view area" is also designated that in some places extends up to 1,525 m from the southernmost tip of the escarpment face. The escarpment is listed in the New Mexico Register of Cultural Properties, and in the National Register of Historic Places. To implement the 3,402–ha conservation plan, cooperation is sought from local landowners and developers and from the state and federal governments. Albuquerque presently owns 293.6 ha, the federal government, 931.5 ha, and the state, 16.2 ha. It is estimated it will cost $80 million to acquire the remaining 2,160.7 ha, which is privately owned. A quarter–cent "quality of life" city sales tax was passed in 1987, and is expected to raise $15 million for land purchase. An additional $15 million will come from general obligation funds and the sale of surplus open space. The state and federal governments are being asked to provide the remaining $50 million. The National Park Service is presently studying the idea of establishing a Petroglyph National Monument, which would require an act of Congress. The state is seeking $2 million worth of land through land trades or by appropriation, and may re–route state–funded roads that impact on the conservation area. Although many issues remain unresolved, the Mayor's office is already working with a landowner's organization in Albuquerque to save areas threatened with imminent development (Siembieda 1987).

In Buffalo, New York

The Tifft Farm Nature Preserve in Buffalo, New York, has been described as an "oasis of wildness surrounded by concrete, pavement and steel" (Gall, undated). This urban reserve was created unconventionally on land reclaimed from a former municipal and industrial waste site, and provides outdoor recreational opportunities to thousands of visitors annually only 4.8 km from downtown Buffalo.

A 107–ha tract of urban waterfront industrial land was purchased by the City of Buffalo in 1972 as additional landfill area. The site, along Lake Erie, had previously served as a dairy farm and stockyard, a transshipment terminal, and a municipal and industrial dump. Despite this abuse, the land had valuable natural features, including a 30–ha marsh, and fish and wildlife resources that were known to local birdwatchers, hunters, and fishermen.

An ad hoc group of citizens, environmentalists, and sportsmen soon developed a conceptual plan to concentrate the dumping area, cover previous dump sites, and create active and passive recreational opportunities on the site. This plan was adopted by the city of Buffalo and its Sewer Authority, and in 1975 steps were taken to begin to restore the area to urban green space that now functions as a wildlife sanctuary, environmental education center, and recreational area. A new lake was developed from a borrow pit, and grasses and legumes, shrubs, and trees were planted to provide food and cover for wildlife. After a decade of allowing the vegetation to "naturalize," the preserve now attracts 175 species of birds; mammals such as fox, deer, and beaver; herptiles, including the blue-spotted salamander; a variety of fish; and many invertebrates.

Bluebird nest boxes, nesting platforms for geese and osprey, brush piles for rabbits, and snags for cavity–dwellers are among the management techniques used at Tifft Farm.

Many school children from the Buffalo area are among those who spend time at the Interpretive Center and on the developed trails each year, and all visitors have the opportunity to participate in nature study, hiking, snowshoeing, cross–country skiing, and other activities.

The Preserve is a department of the Buffalo Museum of Science, and was certified as an Urban Wildlife Sanctuary by the National Institute for Urban Wildlife in 1987 (see the section "Voluntary Registrations" in this report for more information on this national certification program).

The Work of Corporate Enterprise

• One of the largest corporate gifts made to The Nature Conservancy was Consolidation Coal Company's donation of 2,682 ha of surface–mined land in Fulton County, Illinois. More than 75% of the site has been restored to date. Mason Walsh, Chairman of the Conservancy, expressed the appreciation of the organization for this large donation of land, stating, ". . . to our knowledge, [this is] one of the most generous corporate gifts in the history of conservation" (Leedy *et al.* 1987).

• In 1981, the Union Oil Company of California donated a 9.4–ha tract of land to the City of Edmonds, Washington, as a wildlife sanctuary. The area is one of the few freshwater marshes along Puget Sound and is recognized for its sanctuary value by the Washington Department of Game. It is a nesting area for a wide variety of waterfowl and has an appraised value of more than $500,000 (Leedy *et al.* 1985).

• In 1975, a local naturalist brought to the attention of Chevron USA, Inc. officials the presence of the endangered El Segundo blue butterfly on refinery lands in El Segundo, California. Two acres of dunes on the oil company's property were identified as one of the last known habitats of this rare butterfly. The area was immediately fenced and protected as a butterfly sanctuary, and, with the help of a scientist at the University of California, Berkeley, and the U.S. Fish and Wildlife Service, management policies were drawn up by Chevron to protect the El Segundo blue butterfly. The presence of an international airport next to the refinery made the area unattractive to homeowners, and additional land is available on which to transplant the butterfly. Chevron has also sponsored research studies of the insect, and created specific habitat which is attractive to the insects (National Institute for Urban Wildlife 1983, Arnold and Goins 1987).

Rails–to–Trails Conservancy

More than 4,800 km of railroad tracks and railway corridors are abandoned in the U.S. each year. A national organization, the Rails–to–Trails Conservancy, was founded in 1985 to provide legal and technical assistance to help communities preserve these railways for public use. To date, more than 3,800 km of old rail corridors have been converted to 158 multi–purpose trails in 31 states. These so–called "linear parks" are used for recreational activities such as hiking, bicycling, horseback riding, cross–country skiing, birdwatching, and fishing access. Deer and other wildlife are also known to use the trails as corridors. The Conservancy believes a national rail–trail system would help carry out the recommendation of the President's Commission on Americans Outdoors to create a network of Greenways beneficial to people and wildlife, especially in developed areas. Other values of railway conversion include economic stimulation from tourism, natural habitat protection, and historical preservation. (Rails–to–Trails Conservancy 1988).

More on the Nature Conservancy

TNC Management Agreements

The Nature Conservancy sometimes affiliates with state or federal agencies to protect land. In 1985, management agreements were secured with Long Island's Suffolk County and the New York State Office of Parks and Recreation that permit The Nature Conservancy to oversee stewardship of critical natural areas on Long Island. These critical areas are needed to protect piping plovers and other rare, threatened, or endangered species (The Nature Conservancy 1987).

TNC Natural Heritage Program

The Nature Conservancy has set up a data–collection and –retrieval program called the Natural Heritage Program in 43 states, with the goal of cataloging all of the flora and fauna in each state. The species known through existing state records and museum collections are entered into the data base, and then field work by a botanist, zoologist, and ecologist is carried out to verify and expand the data. The information is available to anyone, and may be the most comprehensive national inventory of plants and animals available at this time. Because of the Heritage Program, TNC and other organizations are able to set priorities on the species that need to be protected, and thus, on the location of preserves (Gilbert 1986).

LITERATURE CITED

Adams, L.W. 1988. Some recent advances in urban wildlife research and management. Pages 213–224 *in* R.R. Odom, K.A. Riddleberger, and J.C. Ozier, eds. Proc. Third Southeast. Nongame and Endangered Wildl. Symp. Georgia Dep. Nat. Resour., Social Circle.

Adams, L.W. and A.D. Geis. 1981. Effects of highways on wildlife. Rep. No. FHWA–RD–81–067, Federal Highway Administration, Washington, D.C. 149 pp.

Adams, L.W. and D.L. Leedy, eds. 1987. Integrating man and nature in the metropolitan environment. Natl. Inst. for Urban Wildl., Columbia, Md. 249 pp.

Adams, L.W. and L.E. Dove. 1984. Urban wetlands for stormwater control and wildlife enhancement. Natl. Inst. for Urban Wildl., Columbia, MD. 15 pp.

Adams, L.W., D.L. Leedy, and W.C. McComb. 1987. Urban wildlife research and education in North American colleges and universities. Wildl. Soc. Bull. 15:591–595.

Adams, L.W., L.E. Dove, and D.L. Leedy. 1984. Public attitudes toward urban wetlands for stormwater control and wildlife enhancement. Wildl. Soc. Bull. 12:299–303.

Adams, L.W., L.E. Dove, and T.M. Franklin. 1985a. Mallard pair and brood use of urban stormwater–control impoundments. Wildl. Soc. Bull. 13:46–51.

Adams, L.W., L.E. Dove, and T.M. Franklin. 1985b. Use of urban stormwater control impoundments by wetland birds. Wilson Bull. 97:120–122.

Adams, L.W., T.M. Franklin, L.E. Dove, and J.M. Duffield. 1986. Design considerations for wildlife in urban stormwater management. Trans. North Am. Wildl. and Nat. Resour. Conf. 51:249–259.

Aldrich, J.W. and R.W. Coffin. 1980. Breeding bird populations from forest to suburbia after thirty–seven years. Am. Birds 34:3–7.

American Planning Association. 1980. Bufferyards: their use in performance zoning. PAS Memo, November. 4 pp.

American Planning Association. 1984. L.A. TDRs. Zoning News, November, p. 3.

American Planning Association. 1985. Massachusetts debates land banking bills. Zoning News, May, pp. 3–4.

American Planning Association. 1986. Maryland enacts TDR legislation. Zoning News, September, p. 4.

Anderson, S.H. and C.S. Robbins. 1981. Habitat size and bird community management. Trans. North Am. Wildl. and Nat. Resour. Conf. 46:511–520.

Anonymous. 1987. Americans and the outdoors. Natl. Geographic Soc., Washington, D.C. (A brief summary of the full report of the President's Commission on Americans Outdoors.)

Arnold, R.A. and A.E. Goins. 1987. Habitat enhancement techniques for the El Segundo blue butterfly: an urban endangered species. Pages 173–181 *in* L.W. Adams and D.L. Leedy, eds. Integrating man and nature in the metropolitan environment. Natl. Inst. for Urban Wildl., Columbia, Md.

Aurelia, M.A. 1987. The role of wetland regulation in preserving wildlife habitat in suburban environments. Pages 213–219 *in* L.W. Adams and D.L. Leedy, eds. Integrating man and nature in the metropolitan environment. Natl. Inst. for Urban Wildl., Columbia, Md.

Banks, R.C.. R.W. McDiarmid, and A.L. Gardner. 1987. Checklist of vertebrates of the United States, the U.S. Territories, and Canada. U.S. Fish and Wildl. Serv., Resour. Publ. 166. 79 pp.

Barrett, T.S. 1983. Proposed federal tax regulations. A supplement to T.S. Barrett and P. Livermore (for the Trust for Public Land). 1983. The conservation easement in California. Island Press, Covelo, Calif. 173 pp.

Barrett, T.S. and P. Livermore (for the Trust for Public Land). 1983. The conservation easement in California. Island Press, Covelo, Calif. 173 pp.

Bascietto, J.J. and L.W. Adams. 1983. Frogs and toads of stormwater management basins in Columbia, Maryland. Bull. Md. Herpetol. Soc. 19:58–60.

Batten, L.A. 1972. Breeding bird species diversity in relation to increasing urbanization. Bird Study 19:157–166.

Behrens, J.O. 1972. Tax exemptions and cemeteries. Pages 17–22 *in* E. Finkler. The multiple use of cemeteries. Am. Soc. of Planning Officials, Rep. No. 285. Chicago, Ill.

Beissinger, S.R. and D.R. Osborne. 1982. Effects of urbanization on avian community organization. Condor 84:75–83.

Best, L.B. 1983. Bird use of fencerows: implications of contemporary fencerow management practices. Wildl. Soc. Bull. 11:343-347.

Bezzel, E. 1985. Birdlife in intensively used rural and urban environments. Ornis Fennica 62:90–95.

Blake, J.G. 1986. Species–area relationship of migrants in isolated woodlots in east-central Illinois. Wilson Bull. 98:291–296.

Blake, J.G. and J.R. Karr. 1984. Species composition of bird communities and the conservation benefit of large versus small forests. Biol. Conserv. 30:173–187.

Bond, R.R. 1957. Ecological distribution of breeding birds in the upland forests of southern Wisconsin. Ecol. Monogr. 27:351–384.

Brown, T.L., C.P. Dawson, and R.L. Miller. 1979. Interests and attitudes of metropolitan New York residents about wildlife. Trans. North Am. Wildl. and Nat. Resour. Conf. 44:289–297.

Budd, W.W., P.L. Cohen, P.R. Saunders, and F.R. Steiner. 1987. Stream corridor management in the Pacific Northwest: I. Determination of stream–corridor widths. Environ. Manage. 11:587–597.

Burns, J., K. Stenberg, and W.W. Shaw. 1986. Critical and sensitive wildlife habitats in Tucson, Arizona. Pages 144-150 *in* K. Stenberg and W.W. Shaw, eds. Wildlife conservation and new residential developments. Proc. of a natl. symp. on urban wildl., School of Renewable Nat. Resour., Univ. Arizona, Tucson.

Byrnes, W.R. and H.A. Holt, eds. 1987. Proceedings fourth symposium on environmental concerns in rights–of–way management. Purdue Univ., West Lafayette, Ind. 595 pp.

California Nature Conservancy. Undated. Ring Mountain: room with a view. (Excerpt from a book manuscript in preparation.) San Francisco.

Cassel, J.F. and J.M. Wiehe. 1980. Uses of shelterbelts by birds. Pages 78–87 *in* R.M. DeGraaf and N.G. Tilghman, compilers. Management of western forests and grasslands for nongame birds. USDA For. Serv. Gen. Tech. Rep. INT–86, U.S. Dep. Agric., Forest Service, Ogden, Utah.

Cohen, P.L., P.R. Saunders, W.W. Budd, and F.R. Steiner. 1987. Stream corridor management in the Pacific Northwest: II. Management strategies. Environ. Manage. 11:599–605.

Crabtree, A.F., ed. 1984. Proceedings of the third international symposium on environmental concerns in rights–of–way management. Published by Mississippi State University, Mississippi State.

Davis, A.M. and T.F. Glick. 1978. Urban ecosystems and island biogeography. Environ. Conserv. 5:299–304.

DeGraaf, R.M. 1987. Urban wildlife habitat research— –application to landscape design. Pages 107–111 *in* L.W. Adams and D.L. Leedy, eds. Integrating man and nature in the metropolitan environment. Natl. Inst. for Urban Wildl., Columbia, Md.

DeGraaf, R.M. and J.M. Wentworth. 1981. Urban bird communities and habitats in New England. Trans. North Am. Wildl. and Nat. Resour. Conf. 46:396–413.

Diamond, J.M. 1976. Island biogeography and conservation: strategy and limitations. Science 193:1027–1029.

Dickman, C.R. 1987. Habitat fragmentation and vertebrate species richness in an urban environment. J. Applied Ecol. 24:337-351.

Diehl, J. and T.S. Barrett. 1988. The conservation easement handbook: managing land conservation and historic preservation easement programs. Land Trust Exchange, Alexandria, Va. 269 pp.

Duffield, J.M. 1986. Waterbird use of a urban stormwater wetland system in central California, USA. Colonial Waterbirds 9:227–235.

Emmerich, J.M. and P.A. Vohs. 1982. Comparative use of four woodland habitats by birds. J. Wildl. Manage. 46:43–49.

Faeth, S.H. and T.C. Kane. 1978. Urban biogeography: city parks as islands for Diptera and Coleoptera. Oecologia 32:127–133.

Fahrig, L. and G. Merriam. 1985. Habitat patch connectivity and population survival. Ecology 66:1762–1768.

Farnsworth, N.R. 1988. Screening plants for new medicines. Pages 83–97 *in* E.O. Wilson, ed. Biodiversity. Natl. Acad. Press, Washington, D.C.

Filion, F.L. *et al.* 1983. The importance of wildlife to Canadians: highlights of the 1981 National Survey. Cat. No. CW66–62/1983E, Canadian Wildl. Serv., Ottawa, Ont. 40 pp.

Forman, R.T.T. and M. Godron. 1986. Landscape ecology. J. Wiley and Sons, New York, N.Y. 619 pp.

Franklin, T.M. and J.R. Wilkinson. 1986. Predicted effects on birdlife of two development plans for an urban estate. Pages 105–117 *in* K. Stenberg and W.W. Shaw, eds. Wildlife conservation and new residential developments. School of Renewable Nat. Resour., Univ. Arizona, Tucson.

Gall, W.K. Undated. Breaking the technical barriers: restoration of an urban green space. Buffalo Society of Natural Sciences, Buffalo Museum of Science and Tifft Farm Nature Preserve. Buffalo, N.Y. 5 pp.

Galli, A.E., C.F. Leck, and R.T.T. Forman. 1976. Avian distribution patterns in forest islands of different sizes in central New Jersey. Auk 93:356–364.

Gavareski, C.A. 1976. Relation of park size and vegetation to urban bird populations in Seattle, Washington. Condor 78:375–382.

Geis, A.D. 1974. Effects of urbanization and type of urban development on bird populations. Pages 97–105 *in* J.H. Noyes and D.R. Progulske, eds. A symposium on wildlife in an urbanizing environment. Planning and Resour. Dev. Ser. 28, Holdsworth Nat. Resour. Cent., Univ. of Mass., Amherst.

Geis, A.D. 1986. Planning and design for wildlife conservation in new residential developments--Columbia, Maryland. Pages 67–70 *in* K. Stenberg and W.W. Shaw, eds. Wildlife conservation and new residential developments. School of Renewable Nat. Resour., Univ. Arizona, Tucson.

Gilbert, B. 1986. The Nature Conservancy game. Sports Illustrated, 20 October. Reprinted by The Nature Conservancy.

Gilbert, F.F. 1982. Public attitudes toward urban wildlife: a pilot study in Guelph, Ontario. Wildl. Soc. Bull. 10:245–253.

Goldstein, E.L., M. Gross, and R.M. DeGraaf. 1981. Explorations in bird–land geometry. Urban Ecol. 5:113–124.

Goldstein, E.L., M. Gross, and R.M. DeGraaf. 1983. Wildlife and greenspace planning in medium–scale residential developments. Urban Ecol. 7:201–214.

Halcrow Fox and Associates, Cobham Resource Consultants, and P. Anderson. 1987. Planning for wildlife in metropolitan areas: guidance for the preparation of unitary development plans. Nature Conservancy Council, Northminster House, Peterborough PE1 1UA, U.K. 23 pp.

Hallock, D. 1984. Boulder County makes room for wildlife. Planning 50:12-14.

Hallock, D. 1986. Comprehensive land use planning and wildlife protection in Boulder County, Colorado. Pages 151-155 *in* K. Stenberg and W.W. Shaw, eds. Wildlife conservation and new residential developments. Proc. of a natl. symp. on urban wildl., School of Renewable Nat. Resour., Univ. Arizona, Tucson.

Harris, H.J., Jr., J.A. Ladowski, and D.J. Worden. 1981. Water–quality problems and management of an urban waterfowl sanctuary. J. Wildl. Manage. 45:501–507.

Harris, L. D. 1984. The fragmented forest: island biogeography theory and the preservation of biotic diversity. Univ. Chicago Press, Chicago, Ill. 211 pp.

Harris, L.D. and R.D. Wallace. 1984. Breeding bird species in Florida forest fragments. Proc. Ann. Conf. Southeast. Assoc. Fish & Wildl. Agencies 38:87–96.

Harrison, C., M. Limb, and J. Burgess. 1987. Nature in the city--popular values for a living world. J. Environ. Manage. 25:347–362.

Hench, J.E., K.V. Ness, and R. Gibbs. 1987. Development of a natural resources planning and management process. Pages 29–35 *in* L.W. Adams and D.L. Leedy, eds. Integrating man and nature in the metropolitan environment. Natl. Inst. for Urban Wildl., Columbia, Md.

Hester, F.E. 1985. Statement by the Deputy Director, U.S. Fish and Wildlife Service, Department of the Interior, before the House Subcommittee on Fisheries and Wildlife Conservation and the Environment, Committee on Merchant Marine and Fisheries, on H.R. 1789, to authorize appropriations for four national wildlife refuges.

Hobaugh, W.C. and J.G. Teer. 1981. Waterfowl use characteristics of flood–prevention lakes in north–central Texas. J. Wildl. Manage. 45:16–26.

Hoehne, L.M. 1981. The groundlayer vegetation of forest islands in an urban–suburban matrix. Pages 41–54 *in* R.L. Burgess and D.M. Sharpe, eds. Forest island dynamics in man–dominated landscapes. Springer–Verlag, New York, N.Y.

Houck, M., ed. 1986. The Willamette. Urban Naturalist, Summer issue. Audubon Soc. of Portland, Portland, Oreg.

Houck, M.C. 1987. Urban wildlife habitat inventory: the Willamette River Greenway, Portland, Oregon. Pages 47–51 *in* L.W. Adams and D.L. Leedy, eds. Integrating man and nature in the metropolitan environment. Natl. Inst. for Urban Wildl., Columbia, Md.

Howard, J. 1987. The garden of earthly remains. Horticulture 65:46–56.

Johnson, D., ed. 1987. Alberta Naturalist 17:73–148. (Constituted the proceedings of the Urban Natural Areas Workshop, 24 January 1987, University of Calgary.)

Klein, W.R. 1986. Nantucket tithes for open space. Planning 52:10–13.

Leedy, D.L. 1975. Highway–wildlife relationships: Vol. I, A state–of–the–art report. Rep. No. FHWA–RD–76–4, Federal Highway Administration, Washington, D.C. 183 pp.

Leedy, D.L. 1979. An annotated bibliography on planning and management for urban–suburban wildlife. Rep. No. FWS/OBS–79/25. U.S. Fish and Wildl. Serv., Washington, D.C. 256 pp.

Leedy, D.L. and L.W. Adams. 1982. Wildlife considerations in planning and managing highway corridors. User's manual. Rep. No. FHWA–TS–82–212, Federal Highway Administration, Washington, D.C. 93 pp.

Leedy, D.L. and L.W. Adams. 1984. A guide to urban wildlife management. Natl. Inst. for Urban Wildl., Columbia, Md. 42 pp.

Leedy, D.L. and L.W. Adams. 1986. Wildlife in urban and developing areas: an overview and historical perspective. Pages 8–20 *in* K. Stenberg and W.W. Shaw, eds. Wildlife conservation and new residential developments. School of Renewable Natural Resour., Univ. of Arizona, Tucson.

Leedy, D.L. and L.W. Adams. 1987. The development of urban wildlife programs in the United States. Alberta Naturalist 17:89–104.

Leedy, D.L., L.W. Adams, G.E. Jones, and L.E. Dove. 1987. Environmental reclamation and the coal surface mining industry. Natl. Inst. for Urban Wildl., Columbia, Md. 83 pp.

Leedy, D.L., L.W. Adams, and L.E. Dove. 1985. Environmental conservation and the petroleum industry. Am. Petroleum Inst., Washington, D.C. 47 pp.

Leedy, D.L., L.E. Dove, and T.M. Franklin. 1980. Compatibility of fish, wildlife, and floral resources with electric power facilities and lands: an industry survey analysis. Edison Electric Inst., Washington, D.C. 130 pp.

Leedy, D.L., R.M. Maestro, and T.M. Franklin. 1978. Planning for wildlife in cities and suburbs. Rep. No. FWS/OBS–77/66. U.S. Fish and Wildl. Serv., Washington, D.C. 64 pp.

Leedy, D.L., T.M. Franklin, and E.C. Hekimian. 1975. Highway–wildlife relationships: Vol. II, An annotated bibliography. Rep. No. FHWA–RD–76–5, Federal Highway Administration, Washington, D.C. 417 pp.

Leedy, D.L., T.M. Franklin, and R.M. Maestro. 1981. Planning for urban fishing and waterfront recreation. Rep. No. FWS/OBS–80/35. U.S. Fish and Wildl. Serv., Washington, D.C. 108 pp.

Levenson, J.B. 1981. Woodlots as biogeographic islands in southeastern Wisconsin. Pages 13–39 *in* R.L. Burgess and D.M. Sharpe, eds. Forest island dynamics in man–dominated landscapes. Springer-Verlag, New York, N.Y.

Linehan, J.T., R.E. Jones, and J.R. Longcore. 1967. Breeding–bird populations in Delaware's urban woodlots. Audubon Field Notes 21:641–646.

Luniak, M. 1983. The avifauna of urban green areas in Poland and possibilities of managing it. Acta Ornithologica 19:3–61.

Lyle, J.T. 1987. A general approach to landscape design for wildlife habitat. Pages 87–91 *in* L.W. Adams and D.L. Leedy, eds. Integrating man and nature in the metropolitan environment. Natl. Inst. for Urban Wildl., Columbia, Md.

Lynch, J.F. and R.F. Whitcomb. 1978. Effects of the insularization of the eastern deciduous forest on avifaunal diversity and turnover. Pages 461–489 *in* A. Marmelstein, chairman. Classification, inventory, and analysis of fish and wildlife habitat. Proc. of a Natl. Symp. Rep. No. FWS/OBS–78/76, Fish and Wildl. Serv., USDI, Washington, D.C.

Lyons, J.R. and D.L. Leedy. 1984. The status of urban wildlife programs. Trans. North Am. Wildl. and Nat. Resour. Conf. 49:233-251.

MacArthur, R.H. and E.O. Wilson. 1967. The theory of island biogeography. Princeton Univ. Press, Princeton, N.J. 203 pp.

MacClintock, L., R.F. Whitcomb, and B.L. Whitcomb. 1977. Evidence for the value of corridors and minimization of isolation in preservation of biotic diversity. Am. Birds 31:6–16.

Margules, C., A.J. Higgs, and R.W. Rafe. 1982. Modern biogeographic theory: are there any lessons for nature reserve design? Biol. Conserv. 24:115–128.

Martin, G. 1983. Reserved, forever. PSA Magazine, September. Reprint of the California Nature Conservancy, San Francisco.

Martin, T.E. 1978. Diversity and density of shelterbelt bird communities. M.S. Thesis. South Dakota State Univ., Brookings. 174 pp.

Maryland Department of Natural Resources. 1986. Maryland's Program Open Space. (Concept paper submitted to the President's Commissioin on Americans Outdoors.) Program Open Space, Dep. Nat. Resour., Annapolis.

Maryland Environmental Trust. 1974. Conservation easements. Baltimore. 24 pp.

Matthiae, P.E. and F. Stearns. 1981. Mammals in forest islands in southeastern Wisconsin. Pages 55–66 *in* R.L. Burgess and D.M. Sharpe, eds. Forest island dynamics in man-dominated landscapes. Springer–Verlag, New York, N.Y.

McCabe, R.E., ed. 1988. Transactions of the Fifty-third North American Wildlife and Natural Resources Conference. Wildl. Manage. Inst., Washington, D.C. 621 pp.

Milligan, D.A. 1985. The ecology of avian use of urban freshwater wetlands in King County, Washington. M.S. Thesis, Univ. Washington, Seattle. 145 pp.

Montana Land Reliance. 1979. Conservation law seminar: conservation easements and related charitable conveyances. 20 July. Helena. 93 pp.

Murphy, D.D. 1988. Challenges to biological diversity in urban areas. Pages 71 76 in E.O. Wilson, ed. Biodiversity. Natl. Academy Press, Washington, D.C.

Myers, N. 1988. Tropical forests and their species: going, going...? Pages 28 35 *in* E.O. Wilson, ed. Biodiversity. Natl. Acad. Press, Washington, D.C.

National Institute for Urban Wildlife, undated. The urban wildlife sanctuary program of the National Institute for Urban Wildlife (application for certification). Natl. Inst. for Urban Wildl., Columbia, Md. 8 pp.

National Institute for Urban Wildlife. 1983. Oil company protects El Segundo butterfly. Urban Wildlife News VII(2). Natl. Inst. for Urban Wildl., Columbia, Md.

Naveh, Z. and A.S. Lieberman. 1984. Landscape ecology: theory and application. Springer–Verlag, New York, N.Y. 356 pp.

Nordstrom, S. 1988. Planning for wildlife in cluster housing developments. Draft M.L.A. thesis, Utah State Univ., Logan.

Noss, R.F. 1983. A regional landscape approach to maintain diversity. BioScience 33:700–706.

Noss, R.F. 1987a. Corridors in real landscapes: a reply to Simberloff and Cox. Conserv. Biol. 1:159–164.

Noss, R.F. 1987b. Protecting natural areas in fragmented landscapes. Nat. Areas J. 7:2–13.

Noss, R.F. and L.D. Harris. 1986. Nodes, networks, and MUMs: preserving diversity at all scales. Environ. Manage. 10:299–309.

O'Meara, T.E. 1984. Habitat–island effects on the avian community in cypress ponds. Proc. Ann. Conf. Southeast. Assoc. Fish & Wildl. Agencies 38:97–110.

Penland, S. 1987. The urban wildlife program of the Washington Department of Game. Page 241 *in* L.W. Adams and D.L. Leedy, eds. Integrating man and nature in the metropolitan environment. Natl. Inst. for Urban Wildl., Columbia, Md.

Podoll, E.B. 1979. Utilization of windbreaks by wildlife. Pages 121–127 *in* Windbreak management. Great Plains Agric. Council Publ. 92, Lincoln, Nebr.

Poynton, J.C. and D.C. Roberts. 1985. Urban open space planning in South Africa: a biogeographical perspective. South African J. Sci. 81:33–37.

Progulske, D.R. and D.L. Leedy. 1986. Urban wildlife management: the challenge at home. Trans. North Am. Wildl. and Nat. Resour. Conf. 51:567–572.

Pudelkewicz, P.J. 1981. Visual response to urban wildlife habitat. Trans. North Am. Wildl. and Nat. Resour. Conf. 46:381–389.

Rails–to–Trails Conservancy. 1988. A guide to America's rail–trails. (See also news releases of the Conservancy: 1987, 1988.) 1400 Sixteenth Street, N.W., Washington, D.C. 20036.

Ranney, J.W., M.C. Bruner, and J.B. Levenson. 1981. The importance of edge in the structure and dynamics of forest islands. Pages 67–95 *in* R.L. Burgess and D.M. Sharpe, eds. Forest island dynamics in man–dominated landscapes. Springer–Verlag, New York, N.Y.

Robbins, C.S. 1979. Effect of forest fragmentation on bird populations. Pages 198–213 *in* USDA, Forest Service. Management of north central and northeastern forests for nongame birds. Workshop Proc., U.S. Dep. Agric. For. Serv., Gen. Tech. Rep. NC–51. USDA For. Serv., North Cent. For. Exp. Station, St. Paul, Minn.

Roberts, D.C. and J.C. Poynton. 1985. Central and peripheral urban open spaces: need for biological evaluation. South African J. Sci. 81:464–466.

Salwasser, H. 1987. Greenways for Americans. Pages 119–121 *in* L.W. Adams and D.L. Leedy, eds. Integrating man and nature in the metropolitan environment. Natl. Inst. for Urban Wildl., Columbia, Md.

Schaefer, J.M. 1987. Kansas backyard wildlife certification program. Pages 240–241 *in* L.W. Adams and D.L. Leedy, eds. Integrating man and nature in the metropolitan environment. Natl. Inst. for Urban Wildl., Columbia, Md.

Schauman, S., S. Penland, and M. Freeman. 1987. Public knowledge of and preferences for wildlife habitats in urban open spaces. Pages 113–118 *in* L.W. Adams and D.L. Leedy, eds. Integrating man and nature in the metropolitan environment. Natl. Inst. for Urban Wildl., Columbia, Md.

Schicker, L. 1986. Children, wildlife and residential developments. M.L.A. thesis, North Carolina State Univ., Raleigh. 129 pp.

Schicker, L. 1987. Design criteria for children and wildlife in residential developments. Pages 99–105 *in* L.W. Adams and D.L. Leedy, eds. Integrating man and nature in the metropolitan environment. Natl. Inst. for Urban Wildl., Columbia, Md.

Scott, T.G. and C.H. Wasser. 1980. Checklist of North American plants for wildlife biologists. The Wildlife Society, Washington, D.C. 58 pp.

Shaffer, M.L. 1981. Minimum population sizes for species conservation. BioScience 31:131–134.

Shalaway, S.D. 1985. Fencerow management for nesting birds in Michigan. Wildl. Soc. Bull. 13:302–306.

Shaw, W.W. and V. Supplee. 1987. Wildlife conservation in rapidly expanding metropolitan areas: informational, institutional, and economic constraints and solutions. Pages 191-197 *in* L.W. Adams and D.L. Leedy, eds. Integrating man and nature in the metropolitan environment. Nat. Inst. for Urban Wildl., Columbia, Md.

Shaw, W.W., J.M. Burns, and K. Stenberg. 1986. Wildlife habitats in Tucson: a strategy for conservation. School of Renewable Nat. Resour., Univ. Arizona, Tucson. 17 pp.

Siembieda, W.J. 1987. Rock of ages. Planning 54:28-29.

Sikorowski, L. and S.J. Bissell, eds. 1986. County government and wildlife management: a guide to cooperative habitat development. State Publ. Code DOW-R-M-1-86. Colo. Div. of Wildl., Denver.

Simberloff, D. and J. Cox. 1987. Consequences and costs of conservation corridors. Conserv. Biol. 1:63–71.

Soulé, M.E., *et al.* 1988. Reconstructed dynamics of rapid extinctions of chaparral–requiring birds in urban habitat islands. Conserv. Biol. 2:75–92.

South Carolina Nature Conservancy. 1987. Nature Conservancy protects Botany Bay Island. Press Release, September 29. Columbia. 3 pp.

State of South Carolina, County of Charleston. 1987. Conservation easement (between Barrier Island Preserve, Inc. and The Nature Conservancy). Filed, indexed and recorded: F169-274, September 30, 1987, Charleston County.

Stenberg, K. and W.W. Shaw, eds. 1986. Wildlife conservation and new residential developments: proceedings of a national symposium on urban wildlife. School of Renewable Nat. Resour., Univ. Arizona, Tucson. 203 pp.

Sukopp, H. H.-P. Blume, and W. Kunick. 1979. The soil, flora, and vegetation of Berlin's waste lands. Pages 115–132 *in* I. Laurie, ed. Nature in cities. John Wiley & Sons, Chichester, U.K.

The Nature Conservancy, Connecticut Chapter. Undated. The Connecticut Natural Heritage Registry. Middletown.

The Nature Conservancy, Maryland-Delaware Office. 1988. Maryland Nature Conservancy. Spring Newsletter, Vol. XII, No. 1.

The Nature Conservancy, Vermont Field Office. 1987. Conservationists acquire 295-acre Mud Pond tract. Press Release, 7 August. Montpelier. 2 pp.

The Nature Conservancy. 1987. Annual Report 1986. The Nature Conservancy News 37(2).

Tilghman, N.G. 1987a. Characteristics of urban woodlands affecting breeding bird diversity and abundance. Landscape and Urban Planning 14:481–495.

Tilghman, N.G. 1987b. Characteristics of urban woodlands affecting winter bird diversity and abundance. Forest Ecology and Management 21:163–175.

Tillman, R., ed. 1976. Proceedings of the first national symposium on environmental concerns in rights–of–way management. Published by Mississippi State University, Mississippi State. 335 pp.

Tillman, R.E., ed. 1981. Environmental concerns in rights–of–way management: proceedings of second symposium. Rep. No. EPRI WS–78–141, Electric Power Research Institute, Palo Alto, Calif.

Tiner, R.W., Jr. 1984. Wetlands of the United States: current status and recent trends. U.S. Dep. of the Inter., Fish and Wildl. Serv., Washington, D.C. 59 pp.

Tufts, C. 1987. The National Wildlife Federation's urban wildlife programs...working for the nature of tomorrow. Page 241 *in* L.W. Adams and D.L. Leedy, eds. Integrating man and nature in the metropolitan environment. Natl. Inst. for Urban Wildl., Columbia, Md.

U.S. Department of the Interior, Fish and Wildlife Service and U.S. Department of Commerce, Bureau of the Census. 1985 national survey of fishing, hunting, and wildlife associated recreation. U.S. Gov. Print. Off., Washington, D.C. (in press)

VanDruff, L.W. 1979. Urban wildlife––neglected resource. Pages 184–190 *in* R. Teague and E. Decker, eds. Wildlife conservation: principles and practices. The Wildl. Soc., Washington, D.C.

Vink, A.P.A. 1983. Landscape ecology and land use. Longman Inc., New York, N.Y. 264 pp.

Vizyová A. 1986. Urban woodlots as islands for land vertebrates: a preliminary attempt on estimating the barrier effects of urban structural units. Ecology (CSSR) 5:407–419.

Wacker, J.L. 1987. Land use planning and urban wildlife. Pages 19–21 *in* L.W. Adams and D.L. Leedy, eds. Integrating man and nature in the metropolitan environment. Natl. Inst. for Urban Wildl., Columbia, Md.

Walcott, C.F. 1974. Changes in bird life in Cambridge, Massachusetts from 1860 to 1964. Auk 91:151–160.

Wegner, J.F. and G. Merriam. 1979. Movements by birds and small mammals between a wood and adjoining farmland habitats. J. Appl. Ecol. 16:349–357.

Weller, M.W. 1978. Management of freshwater marshes for wildlife. Pages 267–284 *in* R.E. Good, D.E. Whigham, and R.L. Simpson, eds. Freshwater wetlands: ecological processes and management potential. Proc. of the symp. on freshwater marshes: present status, future needs.

Werner, J.E. and D. Tylka. 1984. Urban biology: the Missouri prototype. *In* W.C. McComb, ed. Proceedings--workshop on management of nongame species and ecological communities. Univ. Kentucky, Lexington.

Whitcomb, R.F., *et al.* 1981. Effects of forest fragmentation on avifauna of the eastern deciduous forest. Pages 125–205 *in* R.L. Burgess and D.M. Sharpe, eds. Forest island dynamics in man–dominated landscapes. Springer–Verlag, New York, N.Y.

Williams, L.R., J. McLauchlin, and T.G. Harrison. 1987. Hedgerows surviving in suburban Kingsbury. The London Naturalist 66:35–39.

Witter, D.J., D.L. Tylka, and J.E. Werner. 1981. Values of urban wildlife in Missouri. Trans. North Am. Wildl. and Nat. Resour. Conf. 46:424–431.

Yahner, R.H. 1982a. Avian use of vertical strata and plantings in farmstead shelterbelts. J. Wildl. Manage. 46:50–60.

Yahner, R.H. 1982b. Microhabitat use by small mammals in farmstead shelterbelts. J. Mamm. 63:440–445.

Yahner, R.H. 1983a. Small mammals in farmstead shelterbelts: habitat correlates of seasonal abundance and community structure. J. Wildl. Manage. 47:74–84.

Yahner, R.H. 1983b. Seasonal dynamics, habitat relationships, and management of avifauna in farmstead shelterbelts. J. Wildl. Manage. 47:85–104.

Appendix A

Scientific Names of Plants and Animals Mentioned in the Text Alphabetized by Common Name for Easy Reference

Plants[a]

Baldcypress, common *(Taxodium distichum)*
Beech *(Fagus spp.)*
Beech, American *(Fagus grandifolia)*
Fern, American maidenhair *(Adiantum pedatum)*
Fern, Virginia grape– *(Botrychium virginianum)*
Hemlock *(Tsuga* spp.*)*
Hickory *(Carya* spp.)
Maple *(Acer* spp.*)*
Maple, sugar *(Acer saccharum)*
Mesquite *(Prosopis* spp.)
Oak *(Quercus* spp.)
Orchid, bracted *(Habenaria viridis)*
Pine *(Pinus* spp.)
Poplar, tulip *(Liriodendron tulipifera)*

Animals[b]

Invertebrates

Butterfly, El Segundo blue *(Euphilotes battoides allyni)*
Spider, blind harvestman *(Sitalcina tiburona)*

Amphibians and Reptiles

Salamander, blue–spotted *(Ambystoma laterale)*
Salamander, four-toed *(Hemidactylium scutatum)*
Turtle, eastern mud *(Kinosternon subrubrum)*
Turtle, loggerhead sea *(Caretta caretta)*
Turtle, red-bellied *(Pseudemys rubriventris)*

Birds

Blackbirds (Icterinae)
Blackbird, red–winged *(Agelaius phoeniceus)*
Bobwhite *(Colinus virginianus)*
Bunting, indigo *(Passerina cyanea)*
Canvasback *(Aythya valisineria)*
Cardinal, northern *(Cardinalis cardinalis)*
Catbird, gray *(Dumetella carolinensis)*
Chat, yellow–breasted *(Icteria virens)*
Chickadee, black–capped *(Parus atricapillus)*
Chickadee, Carolina *(Parus carolinensis)*

Creeper, brown *(Certhia americana)*
Crossbill, white–winged *(Loxia leucoptera)*
Duck, ring–necked *(Aythya collaris)*
Flicker, northern *(Colaptes auratus)*
Flycatchers (Tyrannidae)
Flycatcher, Acadian *(Empidonax virescens)*
Geese (presumably *Branta canadensis)*
Gnatcatcher, blue–gray *(Polioptila caerulea)*
Goose, Canada *(Branta canadensis)*
Grouse, ruffed *(Bonasa umbellus)*
Hawks (Accipitridae)
Hawk, broad–winged *(Buteo platypterus)*
Hawk, red–shouldered *(Buteo lineatus)*
Hawk, red-tailed *(Buteo jamaicensis)*
Heron, great blue *(Ardea herodias)*
Heron, green–backed *(Butorides striatus)*
Jay, blue *(Cyanocitta cristata)*
Killdeer *(Charadrius vociferus)*
Mallard *(Anas platyrhynchos)*
Mockingbird, northern *(Mimus polyglottos)*
Nuthatch, white–breasted *(Sitta carolinensis)*
Osprey *(Pandion haliaetus)*
Ovenbird *(Seiurus aurocapillus)*
Owls (Strigiformes)
Pewee, eastern wood *(Contopus virens)*
Pigeon *(Columba livia)*
Plover, piping *(Charadrius melodus)*
Quail, California *(Callipepla californica)*
Robin, American *(Turdus migratorius)*
Sandpiper, least *(Calidris minutilla)*
Sandpiper, solitary *(Tringa solitaria)*
Sandpiper, spotted *(Actitis macularia)*
Scaup, lesser *(Aythya affinis)*
Sisken, pine *(Carduelis pinus)*
Snipe, common *(Gallinago gallinago)*
Sparrow, house *(Passer domesticus)*
Sparrow, song *(Melospiza melodia)*
Starling *(Sturnus vulgaris)*
Tanager, scarlet *(Piranga olivacea)*
Teal, blue–winged *(Anas discors)*
Thrasher, brown *(Toxostoma rufum)*
Thrasher, California *(Toxostoma redivivum)*
Thrush, wood *(Hylocichla mustelina)*
Titmouse, tufted *(Parus bicolor)*

Towhees (*Pipilo* spp.)
Towhee, rufous–sided *(Pipilo erythrophthalmus)*
Turkey *(Meleagris gallopava)*
Veery *(Catharus fuscescens)*
Vireos (*Vireo* spp.)
Vireo, red–eyed *(Vireo olivaceus)*
Vireo, warbling *(Vireo gilvus)*
Vireo, yellow–throated *(Vireo flavifrons)*
Warblers, wood (Parulinae)
Warbler, black–and–white *(Mniotilta varia)*
Warbler, black–throated green *(Dendroica virens)*
Warbler, Canada *(Wilsonia canadensis)*
Warbler, chestnut–sided *(Dendroica pensylvanica)*
Warbler, hooded *(Wilsonia citrina)*
Warbler, Kentucky *(Oporornis formosus)*
Warbler, worm–eating *(Helmitheros vermivorus)*
Waterthrush, Louisiana *(Seiurus motacilla)*
Woodpecker, red–cockaded *(Picoides borealis)*
Wren, Bewick's *(Thryomanes bewickii)*
Wren, Carolina *(Thryothorus ludovicianus)*
Wren, house *(Troglodytes aedon)*
Wren, winter *(Troglodytes troglodytes)*
Wrentit *(Chamaea fasciata)*
Yellowlegs *(Tringa spp.)*
Yellowthroat, common *(Geothlypis trichas)*

Mammals

Bats (Chiroptera)
Bear, black *(Urus americanus)*
Beaver (presumably *Castor canadensis)*
Bison, woodland *(Bison bison)*
Cat, domestic *(Felis silvestris)*
Coyote *(Canis latrans)*
Deer (presumably *Odocoileus* spp.*)*
Deer, fallow *(Dama dama)*
Deer, roe *(Capreolus capreolus)*
Elk *(Cervus elaphus)*
Fox (presumably *Urocyon cinereoargenteus* or *Vulpes vulpes)*
Fox, gray *(Urocyon cinereoargenteus)*
Lynx *(Lynx canadensis)*
Moles (Talpidae)
Moose *(Alces alces)*
Mouse, white-footed *(Peromyscus leucopus)*

Rabbit (presumably *Sylvilagus floridanus)*
Raccoon *(Procyon lotor)*
Shrews (Soricidae)
Squirrel, Delmarva fox *(Sciurus niger)*
Squirrel, gray *(Sciurus carolinensis)*
Weasels *(Mustela* spp.)
Wolverine *(Gulo gulo)*

[a] According to Scott and Wasser (1980) or referenced author.
[b] According to Banks *et al.* (1987) or referenced author.

Appendix B

Metric Conversions to English Units

Length

     1 cm = 0.394 inches

     1 m = 3.281 feet

     1 km = 0.621 miles

Area

     1 ha = 2.471 acres

Weight

     1 kg = 2.205 pounds

     1 metric ton = 1.102 short tons (2,000 pounds)

Appendix C

Additional Readings

Ambuel, B. and S.A. Temple. 1983. Area–dependent changes in bird communities and vegetation of southern Wisconsin forests. Ecol. 64: 1057–1068.

Arnold, G.W. 1983. The influence of ditch and hedgerow structure, length of hedgerows, and area of woodland and garden on bird numbers of farmland. J. Applied Ecol. 20:731–750.

Arrhenius, O. 1921. Species and area. J. Ecol. 9:95–99.

Baudry, J. 1984. Effects of landscape structure on biological communities: the case of hedgerow network landscapes. Pages 55–65 in J. Brandt and P. Agger, eds. Proceedings of the first international seminar on methodology in landscape ecological research and planning (Vol. 1). Universitetsforlag GeoRuc., Roskilde, Denmark.

Brady, R.F., et al. 1979. A typology for the urban ecosystem and its relationship to larger biogeographical landscape units. Urban Ecol. 4:11–28.

Burgess, R.L. and D.M. Sharpe, eds. 1981. Forest island dynamics in man–dominated landscapes. Springer–Verlag, New York, N.Y. 310 pp.

Burr, R.M. and R.E. Jones. 1968. Influence of parkland habitat management on birds in Delaware. Trans. North Am. Wildl. and Nat. Resour. Conf. 33:299–306.

Butcher, G.S., W.A. Niering, W.J. Barry, and R.H. Goodwin. 1981. Equilibrium biogeography and the size of nature preserves: an avian case study. Oecologia 49:29–37.

Cassola, F. and S. Lovari. 1976. Nature conservation in Italy: proposed national and regional parks and other areas deserving protection. Biol. Conserv. 9:243–257.

Connor, E.F. and E.D. McCoy. 1979. The statistics and biology of the species–area relationship. Am. Nat. 113:791–833.

Dasmann, R.F., J.P. Milton, and P.H. Freeman. 1973. Ecological principles for economic development. John Wiley, New York, N.Y. 252 pp.

DeGraaf, R.M. and J.M. Wentworth. 1981. Urban bird communities and habitats in New England. Trans. North Am. Wildl. and Nat. Resour. Conf. 46:396–413.

Diamond, J.M. 1975. The island dilemma: lessons of modern biogeographic studies for the design of natural reserves. Biol. Conserv. 7:129–146.

Dorney, R.S. and D.W. Hoffman. 1979. Development of landscape planning concepts and management strategies for an urbanizing agricultural region. Landscape Planning 6:151–177.

Faaborg, J. 1979. Qualitative patterns of avian extinction on neotropical land–bridge islands: lessons for conservation. J. Applied Ecol. 16:99–107.

Foresta, R.A. 1980. Elite values, popular values and open space policy. Am. Plan. Assoc. J. 46:449–456.

Forman, R.T.T. 1983. Corridors in a landscape: their ecological structure and function. Ekologia 2:375–387.

Forman, R.T.T. and J. Baudry. 1984. Hedgerows and hedgerow networks in landscape ecology. Environ. Manage. 8:495–510.

Forman, R.T.T. and M. Godron. 1981. Patches and structural components for a landscape ecology. BioScience 31:733–740.

Forman, R.T.T., A.E. Galli, and C.F. Leck. 1976. Forest size and avian diversity in New Jersey woodlots with some land use implications. Oecologia 26:1–8.

Freemark, K.E. and H.G. Merriam. 1986. Importance of area and habitat heterogeneity to bird assemblages in temperate forest fragments. Biol. Conserv. 36:115–142.

Game, M. 1980. Best shape for nature reserves. Nature 287:630–633.

Gill, D. and P. Bonnett. 1973. Nature in the urban landscape: a study of city ecosystems. York Press, Baltimore, Md. 209 pp.

Gilpin, M.E. and J.M. Diamond. 1980. Subdivision of nature reserves and the maintenance of species diversity. Nature 285:567–568.

Goeden, G.B. 1979. Biogeographic theory as a management tool. Environ. Conserv. 6:27–32.

Greater London Council. 1984. Ecology and nature conservation in London. Ecology Handbook No. 1. London, U.K.

Greater London Council. 1985. Nature conservation guidelines for London. Ecology Handbook No. 3. London, U.K.

Greater London Council. 1986. A nature conservation strategy for London: woodland, wasteland, the tidal Thames and two London boroughs. Ecology Handbook No. 4. London, U.K.

Greater Manchester County Council. 1986. A nature conservation strategy for Greater Manchester. Manchester, U.K.

Harris, R.B., L.A. Maguire, and M.L. Shaffer. 1987. Sample sizes for minimum viable population estimation. Conserv. Biol. 1:72–76.

Helle, P. 1984. Effects of habitat area on breeding bird communities in northeastern Finland. Ann. Zool. Fenn. 21:421–425.

Henderson, M.T., G. Merriam, and J. Wegner. 1985. Patchy environments and species survival: chipmunks in an agricultural mosaic. Biol. Conserv. 31:95–105.

Higgs, A.J. and M.B. Usher. 1980. Should nature reserves be large or small? Nature 285:568–569.

Holding, J.H. 1986. Habitat preservation by the private sector: clustered residential developments and TDR's in Teton County, Wyoming. Pages 71–76 *in* K. Stenberg and W.W. Shaw, eds. Wildlife conservation and new residential developments. Proc. Natl. Symp. on Urban Wildl. School of Renewable Nat. Resour., Univ. of Arizona, Tucson.

Hooper, M.D. 1971. The size and surroundings of nature reserves. Pages 555–561 *in* E.D. Duffey and A.S. Watt, eds. The scientific management of animal and plant communities for conservation. Blackwell, Oxford, U.K.

IUCN. 1980. World conservation strategy. Living resource conservation for sustainable development. IUCN, Gland, Switzerland.

Kindlmann, P. 1983. Do archipelagoes really preserve fewer species than one island of the same total area [sic]. Oecologia 59:141–144.

Kitchener, D.J., J. Dell, and B.G. Muir. 1982. Birds in western Australian wheatbelt reserves—implications for conservation. Biol. Conserv. 22:127–163.

LaCava, J. and J. Hughes. 1984. Determining minimum viable population levels. Wildl. Soc. Bull. 12:370–376.

Lehmkuhl, J.F. 1984. Determining size and dispersion of minimum viable populations for land management planning and species conservation. Environ. Manage. 8:167–176.

Lewis, P. 1967. Regional design for human impact. U.S. Dep. Inter., Natl. Park Serv., Northeast Region, Madison, Wis.

Lewis, T. 1969a. The distribution of flying insects near a low hedgerow. J. Applied Ecol. 6:443–452.

Lewis, T. 1969b. The diversity of the insect fauna in a hedgerow and neighboring fields. J. Applied Ecol. 6:453–458.

Lovari, S. and F. Cassola. 1975. Nature conservation in Italy: the existing natural parks and other protected areas. Biol. Conserv. 8:127–141.

Love, D., J.A. Grzybowski, and F.L. Knopf. 1985. Influence of various land uses on windbreak selection by nesting Mississippi kites. Wilson Bull. 97:561–565.

Lussenhop, J. 1977. Urban cemeteries as bird refuges. The Condor 79:456–461.

Lynch, J.F. and D.F. Whigham. 1984. Effects of forest fragmentation on breeding bird communities in Maryland USA. Biol. Conserv. 28:287–324.

Maguire, C.C. 1987. Incorporation of tree corridors for wildlife movement in timber areas: balancing wood production with wildlife habitat management. J. Wash. Acad. Sci. 77:193–199.

Martin, T.E. 1980. Diversity and abundance of spring migratory birds using habitat islands on the Great Plains. Condor 82:430–439.

Martin, T.E. 1981. Limitation in small habitat islands: chance or competition? Auk 98:715–733.

May, R.M. 1975. Island biogeography and the design of wildlife preserves. Nature 254:177–178.

McHarg, I.L. 1969. Design with nature. Natural History Press, Garden City, N.Y. 197 pp.

Merriam, G. 1984. Connectivity: a fundamental characteristic of landscape pattern. Pages 5–15 *in* J. Brandt and P. Agger, eds. Proceedings of the first international seminar on methodology in landscape ecological research and planning (Vol. 1). Universitetsforlag GeoRuc., Roskilde, Denmark.

Møller, A.P. 1987. Breeding birds in habitat patches: random distribution of species and individuals? J. Biogeogr. 14:225–236.

Moore, N.W. and M.D. Hooper. 1975. On the number of bird species in British woods. Biol. Conserv. 8:239–250.

Opdam, P.D. van Dorp, and C.J.F. ter Braak. 1984. The effect of isolation on the number of woodland birds in small woods in the Netherlands. J. Biogeogr. 11:473–478.

Petrides, G.A. 1942. Relation of hedgerows in winter to wildlife in central New York. J. Wildl. Manage. 6:261–280.

Pickett, S.T.A. and P.S. White. 1985. The ecology of natural disturbance and patch dynamics. Academic Press, San Diego, Calif. 472 pp.

Picton, H.D. 1979. The application of insular biogeographic theory to the conservation of large mammals in the northern Rocky Mountains. Biol. Conserv. 15:73–79.

Pollard, E., M.D. Hooper, and N.W. Moore. 1974. Hedges. Taplinger Publ. Co., New York, N.Y.

Pollard, E. and J. Relton. 1970. Hedges. V. A study of small mammals in hedges and cultivated fields. J. Appl. Ecol. 7:549–557.

Rafe, R.W., M.B. Usher, and R.G. Jefferson. 1985. Birds on reserves: the influence of area and habitat on species richness. J. Appl. Ecol. 22:327–335.

Raphael, M.G. 1984. Wildlife populations in relation to stand age and area in Douglas–fir forests of northwestern California. Pages 259–274 *in* W.R. Meehan, T.R. Merrell, Jr., and T.A. Hanley, eds. Fish and wildlife relationships in old–growth forests: proceedings of a symposium held in Juneau, Alaska, 12–15 April 1982. Am. Inst. Fish. Res. Biol.

Reed, J.M., P.D. Doerr, and J.R. Walters. 1986. Determining minimum population sizes for birds and mammals. Wildl. Soc. Bull. 14:255–261.

Reed, T.M. 1983. The role of species–area relationships in reserve choice: a British example. Biol. Conserv. 25:263–271.

Robbins, C.S. 1980. Effect of forest fragmentation on breeding bird populations in the Piedmont of the Mid-Atlantic region. Atlantic Nat. 33:31–36.

Rosenberg, K.V. and M.G. Raphael. 1986. Effects of forest fragmentation on vertebrates in Douglas–fir forests. Pages 263–272 *in* J. Verner, M.L. Morrison, and C.J. Ralph, eds. Wildlife 2000: modeling habitat relationships of terrestrial vertebrates. The Univ. of Wisconsin Press, Madison.

Rusterholz, K.A. and R.W. Howe. 1979. Species–area relations of birds on small islands in a Minnesota lake. Evolution 33:468–477.

Simberloff, D.S. and L.G. Abele. 1976. Island biogeography theory and conservation practice. Science 191:285–286.

Simberloff, D.S. and L.G. Abele. 1982. Refuge design and island biogeographic theory: effects of fragmentation. Am. Nat. 120:41–50.

Soulé, M.E., ed. 1986. Conservation biology: the science of scarcity and diversity. Sinauer Assoc., Inc., Sunderland, Mass. 584 pp.

Soulé, M.E. and D. Simberloff. 1986. What do genetics and ecology tell us about the design of nature reserves? Biol. Conserv. 35:19–40.

Soulé, M.E. and B.A. Wilcox, eds. 1980. Conservation biology: an evolutionary–ecological perspective. Sinauer Assoc., Inc., Sunderland, Mass. 395 pp.

Spirn, A.W. 1984. The granite garden: urban nature and human design. Basic Books, Inc., New York, N.Y. 334 pp.

Terborgh, J. 1975. Faunal equilibria and the design of wildlife preserves. Pages 369–379 *in* F.B. Golley and E. Medina, eds. Tropical ecological systems: trends in terrestrial and aquatic research. Springer–Verlag, New York, N.Y.

Vilkitis, J. 1978. Wildlife habitat as an integral component of a planned unit development. Urban Ecol. 3:171–187.

West Midlands County Council. 1984. The nature conservation strategy for the County of West Midlands. Birmingham, U.K.

Whitcomb, R.F., J.F. Lynch, P.A. Opler, and C.S. Robbins. 1976. Island biogeography and conservation: strategy and limitations. Science 193: 1030–1032.

White, P.S. 1987. Natural disturbance, patch dynamics, and landscape pattern in natural areas. Nat. Areas J. 7:14–22.

Whitney, G.C. and W.J. Somerlot. 1985. A case study of woodland continuity and change in the American midwest. Biol. Conserv. 31:265–287.

Williamson, M. 1975. The design of wildlife preserves. Nature (London) 256:519.

Wright, D.F. 1977. A site evaluation scheme for use in the assessment of potential nature reserves. Biol. Conserv. 11:293–305.

Yahner, R.H. 1985. Effects of forest fragmentation on winter bird abundance in central Pennsylvania. Proc. Pa. Acad. Sci. 59:114–116.